3 PENDULUM LANGUAGES

Contact your Angelic Team, Pendulum on the Hand & Charts and Maps

Raven Shamballa
M.S. Counseling, Spiritual Teacher, Pranic Healer, Hypnotherapist

Copyright © 2019 Raven Shamballa.

All rights reserved. No part of this book may be used or reproduced by any means, graphic, electronic, or mechanical, including photocopying, recording, taping or by any information storage retrieval system without the written permission of the author except in the case of brief quotations embodied in critical articles and reviews.

Balboa Press books may be ordered through booksellers or by contacting:

Balboa Press
A Division of Hay House
1663 Liberty Drive
Bloomington, IN 47403
www.balboapress.com
1 (877) 407-4847

Because of the dynamic nature of the Internet, any web addresses or links contained in this book may have changed since publication and may no longer be valid. The views expressed in this work are solely those of the author and do not necessarily reflect the views of the publisher, and the publisher hereby disclaims any responsibility for them.

The author of this book does not dispense medical advice or prescribe the use of any technique as a form of treatment for physical, emotional, or medical problems without the advice of a physician, either directly or indirectly. The intent of the author is only to offer information of a general nature to help you in your quest for emotional and spiritual well-being. In the event you use any of the information in this book for yourself, which is your constitutional right, the author and the publisher assume no responsibility for your actions.

Any people depicted in stock imagery provided by Getty Images are models,
and such images are being used for illustrative purposes only.
Certain stock imagery © Getty Images.

ISBN: 978-1-9822-2774-6 (sc)
ISBN: 978-1-9822-2775-3 (e)

Library of Congress Control Number: 2019906526

Print information available on the last page.

Balboa Press rev. date: 05/14/2019

Other Books by Raven Shamballa

An Illustrated Guide to the 7 Primary Chakras

Receive a Free E-Book Download. This E-book presents an illustrated guide to the 7 Primary Chakras. These images are meant to be a learning tool for understanding the emotional and energetic poles of the chakras. Each of the 7 Primary Chakras have psychological themes and express both positive and negative emotions and energetic moods and behaviors.

In the table that accompanies the illustrations, I provide affirmations you can use with each chakra to open and balance the chakras. There is a quick reference listing the Attributes or Characteristics to the 7 chakras. There is a table where you can easily determine if a chakra is in balance or out of balance. This is a great learning tool to help you learn more about the 7 Primary Chakras.

For a free download of An Illustrated Guide to the 7 Primary Chakras, please visit www.ravenlightbody.com

The 100 Chakra Book, An Introduction to Negative Energy Release Work

This is the foundation teaching material for Raven energy healing practice Negative Energy Release Work (NERW). Raven introduces the concept that humans have 100 chakras, and advanced souls have up to 500 chakras. In the 100 Chakra book, Raven gives a detailed explanation of the 7 Primary Charkas, The Higher Chakras and the Ascending Chakras. She discusses the similarities and differences in the energy body and the soul body, and dives into exoteric concepts of the Higherself, and consciousness. She touches on developing your psychic abilities and working with your angelic team.

NERW has an emphasis on removing negative energies from the energy body, while expanding the soul body in meditation. A self-study, self-healing course is offered in the book to familiarize you with the concepts of the work.

To receive a free energy healing self-study course on the 100 Chakra System, please visit www.ravenlightbody.com

The 3 Pendulum Languages

In this book, Raven explains how you can use the Pendulum to start communicating with your white light angelic team. Raven teaches how to contact your angelic team and start communicating with them. Raven's pendulum on the hand language gives a detail explanations of how you can advance your pendulum practice from simple Yes/No/Maybe questions to developing conversations with your team. Raven also explains techniques for working with charts and maps to receive more information.

The 3 Pendulum Languages contains 15 pendulum charts to assist you in conceptualizing a new way to receive information from your angels. Blank charts are provided for you to start your own journey into using this divination tool. Using the pendulum as a tool for angel communication is discusses as a training tool to help develop clairaudience, the ability to hear messages from your angels.

To receive a free download of the Angel Pendulum Chart, go to www.ravenlightbody.com

The 10 Cosmic Dimensions, A Spiritual Guidebook to Ascension

In the book, The 10 Cosmic Dimensions, A Spiritual Guidebook to Ascension, Raven shares information she has received from her guides and the Ascended Masters. She explains the concepts of karma, past lives, life between lives and the Light Realms. The cosmic dimensional scale is a measure of human spiritual evolution. Understanding where you are on the scale and in relationship to other people helps to give insight as to your spirit growth and how to interact with others, especially those lower on the cosmic dimensional scale.

This book includes a self-study course with 10 worksheets to assist you in understanding where you are on the scale.

To receive a free chapter, visit www.ravenlightbody.com

Chakra Balancing with the Pendulum

In the book, Chakra Balancing with the Pendulum, Raven explores the language of the pendulum when working with the 7 Primary Chakras. This book teaches how to read your own chakras and how to balance them. It also gives information on how to read clients' chakras and assist them to balance. Certification courses in Negative Energy Release Work and Chakra Balancing will be taught in the future.

For a free download, go to www.ravenlightbody.com

For more information on these topics stay connected!

YouTube: Raven Shamballa

Facebook: Raven Lightbody

Instagram: ravenshamballalightbody

Pinterest: ravenlightbody

About The Author

In 2014, Raven Shamballa awoke from an operation to find she was a full-blown psychic. After recovered from surgery, she recalled a vision of traveling to the Light Realms and hearing from her Counsel of Masters. She was told by her Counsel of Masters that her psychic gifts would be advanced so she could bring forward a new system of energy healing called Negative Energy Release Work (NERW) and create this book defining the 100 Chakras.

Raven lives in Oceanside CA, where she works as an energy healer, psychic and psychotherapist. She continues to write books, lead meditation and expand the content of this work online. For more information, see her website - www.ravenlightbody.com, search 'Raven Shamballa' on YouTube, search 'Raven Lightbody' on Facebook, or find 'ravenshamballalightbody' on Instagram.

Readings are available by phone or in person in Oceanside CA, or cities she visits. Psychic readings include past lives, finding your life purpose, angel names, relationship issues, advancing in spiritual practice, psychic development and galactic origins. Negative Energy Release Work is an energy healing technique taught by Raven. For more information on classes and workshops visit her website.

Raven grew up as Monica Kelly in Clovis, CA. Her parents were immigrants. Her mom was born in Rio de Janeiro, Brazil and her father was born in Calcutta, India. After he was converted at a Billy Graham crusade, her father decided to become a Christian minister in America. Raven grew up within a strong Christian faith.

In college, Raven decided to practice hatha yoga to explore her Indian roots. That led to countless workshops on the subject of metaphysics. During this time she lived in a yoga community which introduced her to meditation, Kriya yoga and Raja Yoga. She returned to Fresno for graduate school. She graduated as a Marriage and Family Therapist at California State University Fresno in 2008. After graduation she discovered energy work, spiritual hypnosis and past life regression.

After the psychic opening, a direct connection was established with her angelic team, allowing her to pursue this work of teaching about the energy body and helping others open their psychic gifts.

Acknowledgements

Thank you to my former husband John Kelly for all his love and support during the process of writing this book. I appreciate his encouraging words to follow my path, take charge of my career, and to be independent and strong. His support allowed me time to meditate, spiritually seek and grow in my wisdom. We had a beautiful relationship.

I want to thank my mom, Sonia Patnaik. She has been there over the years watching me grow and evolve on my path. Although my work in spiritual hypnosis has challenged her, she too listened to my stories. She was there when I went through my operation and psychic awakening. She has witnessed my growth in the light and has been there for me.

I thank all my yoga instructors. I am in gratitude to the Seattle Ananda Community, for all I learned during my stay there in the yoga community. I want to thank Dr. Garcia at California State University of Fresno for his support during my time in studying to be a Marriage and Family Therapist. He gave me the freedom to be a spiritualist within the framework of western psychology.

Thank you to all the support staff that had a hand in putting this book together. To my son, Darshan Davis.

Thank you again, Divine Source and the Ascended Masters. I am profoundly humbled and grateful for this mission. May we wake up as many people as possible. May Lightworkers everywhere learn to directly connect to Divine Source to ask their own questions and receive their own answers. Let us bring light to the world!

Table of Contents

Chapter 1. Using the Pendulum to Communicate with the Guides 9
  Introducing the 3 Pendulum Languages 9
  What Makes the Pendulum Move? 10
  State Your Intentions Clearly 10
  Why Do I Get Bad Answers? 11
  Using the Pendulum to Develop Clairaudience & Telepathy 12
  Am I Making the Pendulum Move? Developing Telekinesis 12
  Why Can't I Make the Pendulum Move? 13

Chapter 2. Pendulum Precautions 14
  Is Working with the Pendulum Dangerous? 14
  How I Developed Spiritual Confidence 15
  Ascension Evolution 15
  Interference 16
  Protocol for Using the Pendulum 16

Chapter 3. Pendulum Basics 19
  How to Hold the Pendulum 19
  What Type of Pendulum Should I Use? 20
  What if I Have Programed My Pendulum in a Different Way? 21

Chapter 4. Contacting your Angelic Team 22
  Create a Sacred Space 22
  The Line of Questioning 23
  Questions to Avoid 24
  Giving a Reading with the Pendulum 25
  Humans and Guides Have Different Perspectives 26

Chapter 5. More Information on Your Angelic Team 27
  How I Met My Angelic Team 27
  The Difference between Angels and Guides 28
  Younger Souls and Advanced Souls 29
  How Many Angels are in my Field? 30
  Call In More Protection and Clearing Angels 31

Chapter 6. Learn the Names of Your Angels 33
  Naming Angels and Guides 33
  3 Pendulum Charts for Meeting Your Angelic Team 34
  Types of Angels and Guides 35
  Additional Purposes for Using the Number and Alphabet Charts 36
  More Questions to Ask When Learning the Names of Your Angels 37
  Numbers Chart 38
  Alphabet Chart 39
  Angel Types Pendulum Key 40
  Angel Types Chart 42

Chapter 7. Pendulum on the Hand **44**
    How the Pendulum Language Developed 44
    Programming the Pendulum on the Hand 45
    Orientation, Yes, No, Not Really, Not Yet 45
    Not Ready to Tell You, No Comment 47
    Certainly, Assign Names and Items to Your Fingers 48
    Scaling Questions 50
    Numbers on the Hand 51
    Time Marks on the Hand 52
    Pendulum on The Hand Chart (1-3) 54
    Pendulum on The Hand Chart (4-6) 55
    Pendulum on The Hand Chart (7-9) 56
    Pendulum on The Hand Chart (10-12) 57

Chapter 8. Making Conversation with your Angelic Team **58**
    Guides Want Us to Take the Lead 58
    Using the Pendulum Conversation Style 59
    Feeling for the Conversation 59
    Example Conversation 1. Should I go back to school? 60
    Example Conversation 2. What workshop should I take? 61
    Example Conversation 3. What happened last night in dreamtime? 62
    Example Conversation 4. What vitamins or supplements should I take? 63
    Free Will and Choice 64
    Feeling for Your Guides 64

Chapter 9. What Kind of Questions Should I Ask? **66**
    Life Path Questions 66
    Life Purpose & Career Questions 68
    Relationship Questions 69
    Metaphysical Questions 71
    Asking "How" or "Why" Questions 73

Chapter 10. Health, Healing Questions & Charts **74**
    Vitamins and Herbs 75
    Questions to Ask About Vitamins and Herbs 76
    Nutrition and Exercise 78
    Questions to Ask About Nutrition and Exercise 80
    Crystal & Essential Oil 82
    Questions to Ask About Crystals 82
    Questions to Ask About Essential Oils 84
    Blank Charts 86
    Creative Charts 86

Chapter 11. Maps & Diagrams **90**
    Working with Maps and Diagrams 90
    Technique for Casting the Pendulum 91
    Notes 96

Chapter 1. Using the Pendulum to Communicate with the Guides

Introducing the 3 Pendulum Languages

This book overviews the correct use of the pendulum for white light spirit communication. As many lightworkers grow on the spiritual path, they naturally gravitate towards divination tools. A pendulum is a weighted object hanging from a string. If you hold it and allow the pendulum to dangle, and then ask it a question, the pendulum moves.

After the first time I picked up the pendulum, I was fascinated with the instrument. I was definitely not moving it consciously. I was very curious and started asking questions. After a few weeks, I became bored with yes/no questions and answers. I started to study the subject, and found out there were many ways to use the pendulum.

I began wanting to know my angel's name. Then I wanted to know how many angels were on my team. Then I wanted to know what tasks they helped me with. Once I knew my angels' names, I started addressing them by name when I used the pendulum. I could hold different conversations with each one. I wanted to know how long they had been working with me. Had I known them before I was born? Were there also guides and if so how many? I was profoundly curious once I made contact with my angelic team.

Then I started using the pendulum after I taught a yoga class. I would hold the pendulum over people's chakras after yoga to demonstrate the spin of their chakras. Then I started checking people's chakras prior to class, to show the differences in the energy spin of the chakra before and after class. Occasionally, the pendulum would make a specific swing I didn't understand. I would go home to channel to understand what my guides were trying to show me.

From the beginning of my study I used pendulum charts. I used the alphabet chart and number chart to get all kinds of information. I found there was a skill in how you asked the questions, and also what kind of questions to ask. I started with Yes/No/Maybe charts but quickly graduated from that. I began to make marks on the charts. I would tell my guides what the marks meant to me and then they would start using the marks. Then it occurred to me I could make my own chart.

Over time, 3 pendulum languages developed. These languages allowed for advanced communication with the spirit realms.

I am excited to share these 3 pendulum languages. When you start to develop communication with your angelic team, the relationship grows and develops. This is an exciting time for lightworkers. No one will sit on the bench, your life purpose is important and a mission will come to you. Everyone is needed and everyone is here on purpose. It's an exciting day, the first time a lightworker makes the pendulum move. If you can get the pendulum to move without much effort, that means you have aptitude to channel and develop a relationship with your guides that will serve you on your journey.

The first language
discusses how to contact your angelic team.

The second language
is pendulum on the hand. This assisted me in getting the information quickly, and eventually led to "tapping" on the hand, which is a more advanced skill and much faster than using the pendulum.

The third language
covers working with charts and maps. Blank charts are provided in this book to help you develop your own conversation with your angelic team.

What Makes the Pendulum Move?

There are many methods for asking Yes/No questions. I have learned these methods taking casual weekend workshops. Many people are familiar with muscle testing. Many chiropractors use muscle testing in their practice as a way to test for nutritional deficiencies. In that case, "the body" is responding to a stimulant which produces a strong muscle or a weaker muscle. If the muscle is strong, the test result is a "yes" answer. If the muscle is weak, the test result is a "no" answer.

There is the finger trick, which I have seen many people use. With the non-dominant hand, left for most of us, touch your thumb to your index finger, which makes a circle. Using the pointer finger of the dominant hand, right for most of us, try to break the circle. This is easy to do. Next, ask an easy yes/or no question, for example, I am a female? If the index finger stays in the circle the answer is yes, if the index finger breaks the circle the answer is no. If you are a female and the answer is yes, your pointer finger won't break the circle. If you are a male, and the answer is no, the pointer finger will easily break the circle.

Most people that use the pendulum start by asking Yes/No/Maybe questions. This is a simple way to get information. But asking Yes/No/Maybe questions is completely different than developing a style of communication in which you can dialogue and hold a conversation with your angelic team.

If we start using the pendulum as a language for spirit contact we are moving into a different arena. It is important to ask "What makes the pendulum move? Who is moving the pendulum and what is giving me the answers?" What I have learned from teaching pendulum is just because you are skilled enough to get the pendulum to move, doesn't mean you are necessarily channeling your white light angelic team.

Using the pendulum for spirit communication is a form of divination work and a way to channel entities that are not present in a physical form. The answer to the question, "What makes the pendulum move?" becomes complex. Angels, spirit guides, the Higherself, your own conscious mind, negative energy, lost souls, and both positive and negative galactics are all examples of astral entities that can be channeled.

The pendulum is a communication tool you can use to navigate in the spirit realm, but it also comes with a few precautions which I overview in this opening section. After all, we are working in the invisible realms. Novices, especially, might track down a path where they think they are communicating with their guides only to end up with poor results or answers to questions they know are not true.

State Your Intentions Clearly

Many people who work with the pendulum are not clear about their intentions. Many students have not made a strong intention about who they are attempting to communicate with. As they work with the pendulum, they get bad answers. Or the pendulum swings only clockwise to every question. They may get mixed messages with the pendulum. The pendulum feels inconsistent and confused. Discouraged, they put it down.

As one advances on their spiritual path, many lightworkers are called to energy healing and divination work and want to communicate with their angelic team. If you are reading this book, you are a lightworker. A lightworker is a generalized term, meaning someone who wants to bring light to the dark world. Lightworkers are usually on their own spiritual path, rather than following traditional religions. Often they are advanced souls, and have volunteered to be here serving humanity during this difficult time of transition.

In this teaching, the strong intention is that one is attempting to communicate with their angelic team. Your angelic team is the total number of angels and spirit guides that are working with you to accomplish your life goals. This team will include one or more Ascended Masters, which are also called Lords of Love. The team also includes your Higherself, which is aware of your life purpose. Usually one to four spirit guides take a leadership role in working with you. The guides start by producing number synchronicities and other angel signs. All information you are receiving is for your greatest good and coming from love and light.

If you have seen number signals like 444 or 1111, that means you are a candidate. A candidate is known to the guides in one of two ways. A candidate is either an advanced soul that has volunteered to do a mission on Earth or they are a younger soul that is excited about healing and helping other people and have asked with a sincere heart to do the work. There are many advanced souls out there that have not yet become conscious of who they really are, beyond this lifetime, and what their potential is.

If you are unsure if you are a candidate or not, just make a formal prayer request, asking for more information and tell them you want to be of service in the world. You will receive guidance. Your angelic team is listening and you will be heard. Many people tell me they see angel signs but don't know what their guides want them to do. If you are seeing angel signs it means it's time to get to work. They want you to become aware of your potential as a healer or helper in the world. Sign up for a new class, find a life coach, study energy healing or practice yoga. It won't be long before a new period of growth will come to you.

Several lightworkers want to "channel" or communicate with the spirit world. Channeling defines a broad category of techniques that are used for communication with the spirit realm.

This book teaches specifically how to use the pendulum as a channeling tool to receive information from your white light angelic team.

In some cases, lightworkers may be called to mediumship. Mediumship is the ability to channel departed love ones and to assist lost souls in crossing over to the other side. The pendulum can act as a communication device for mediumship once you reach an advanced level and know with confidence that you have been called to do the work.

Know that as you move through this material, all the information is coming from Divine sources of love and light. Intend that all divination work assists to build a relationship with your angelic team. The purpose of the relationship is for healing, staying on path, and reaching your spiritual goals. Ask that all information you receive be for the purpose of healing yourself and then healing others. Intend to only work with the light and be protected from all negative energies. Ask that all information received is for your greatest good and highest happiness. And choose an Ascended Master for your path. There can be one or many. Follow your inner guidance.

Why Do I Get Bad Answers?

If you can make the pendulum move but you sometimes get bad answers, there are a few reasons why this is occurring. First, you are not channeling an angel or spirit guide, you are channeling a neutral or negative energy. You may also be channeling a lost soul. The second reason is that you are not clear enough to channel your angelic team. "Clear enough to channel" is a phrase that implies you need to take some time to clear your energy field and meditate prior to attempting to channel, especially with the pendulum. This insures that you remove all negative energies from your field and your chakra system, which can cause interference when people are trying to connect with their angels.

The concepts of energy healing, clearing, negative energies and lost souls are discussed in my book the 100 Chakra System. This book defines 100 chakras and discusses types of negative energies. The 100 Chakra System book is the foundational book for the 3 Pendulum Languages. Many of the concepts I mention here are discussed at length in the 100 Chakra System book.

This book discusses the importance of clearing the energy body of negative energy and drawing in white light energy to achieve optimal balance. Spiritual practice and purification assure you grow in the work of channeling angels. An energy healing and meditation practice are recommended to help you cleanse and be a clear channel for the light.

Another reason you might get bad answers is that you are too emotionally invested in the line of questioning to get a correct answer. For example, take the classic question, "Should I breakup with my boyfriend?" In order to receive a clear answer you have to be emotionally clear and feeling grounded. Your changing emotions, day to day, would create interference with the answer. Or you may not like the answer to the question, and therefore get mixed signals. If you need an answer and are very confused or emotional, it is best to find a reader who is neutral about the situation that can counsel you from a neutral position.

Another reason for getting bad answers is an incorrect line of questioning. In our example about the bad break-up, other questions that often follow are, "Is he cheating on me?" "Does he like someone else?" "Should I break up with him?" This line of questioning is not the most appropriate line of questioning from a guidance point of view. This line of questioning pulls from insecurities and worry. As we move through the pendulum languages, I give more suggestions on how to ask questions. In this example, when people ask me this question, I always re-phrase the question, "Has the relationship served its purpose?"

Using the Pendulum to Develop Clairaudience & Telepathy

The most important role of the pendulum is to provide a tool to assist the student in learning clairaudience & telepathy. Clairaudience is the ability to hear your guides, or receive information from them. Telepathy is knowing a communication before it's spoken, or in this case, before the pendulum shows the answer.

Using the pendulum is the first step in opening lines of communication with your spirit team. As you progress and become more confident the goal should be to hear your guides internally, or just know the answer intuitively.

Using the pendulum is like using training wheels. You only need the training wheels until you learn how to ride the bike. In the beginning, as you learn how to work with the divination tool, you are waiting and watching for the pendulum to give you the answer. As you develop the practice of asking questions and waiting for the swing to present the answer, you start to anticipate or know the answer. Eventually, some lightworkers will start to hear the answer internally. As you advance in the practice you will know the answer before the pendulum has a chance to complete its swing. When this happens, you know you are developing quickly. Eventually you put the pendulum down, you can know or hear the answer ahead of the swing.

Am I Making the Pendulum Move? Developing Telekinesis

The pendulum is an instrument that can receive a thought communication. A thought produces an electro-chemical pulse through the energy body. The thoughts are given by some 3rd party and then that pulse travels through the energy body until it reaches the hand and moves the pendulum. The pendulum receives the impulse and shows the answer.

This brings us back to the question, who moves the pendulum? Who or what is sending the thoughts or pulses through the energy body? Can one direct the pendulum to move? The answer is, Yes! Indeed you can make the pendulum move with your mind. In that case you are not performing spirit contact or channeling, instead you are working on developing telekinesis. Telekinesis is the ability to move an object with your mind. The easiest tool to begin practicing this skill is using your conscious mind to make the pendulum move.

In fact as you learn the pendulum, one of the exercises is to practice making it move with your mind. Your consciousness is like a spark of light, it moves to wherever you place your attention. Your intention can create enough energy to make the pendulum move as you command it. If you are working the pendulum on your hand, and you think, "move to pointer finger", that thought pulse moves along a channel, from your thought intention in your mind to the pendulum. If you "intend" to move the pendulum and it moves, then you know you made it move.

Practicing to move the pendulum with your mind is helpful to create those patterns of movement. In this way you are practicing swinging the pendulum with your mind. With spirit contact, you ask a question you don't know the answer to and the instrument gives you a response, then you know you received an answer from a guide. The guide's answer creates an impulse that traveled through the energy body to the dominant hand holding the pendulum and you receive an answer.

It is very exciting when you can move the pendulum with your mind and it is worthwhile to practice. It clearly demonstrates the power of "intention". If you can move an object with your intention, then what else in our reality can you move with your mind? The power of "intention" is demonstrated as you move the pendulum with your mind.

Why Can't I Make the Pendulum Move?

There are some people who have a hard time getting the pendulum to move in the first place. They try and nothing happens. Why is it that some people can get the pendulum to move and other people cannot? There are two answers. The first is, there is not enough energy flow in the person's body. The second answer is the person is not yet ready to channel using the pendulum and their higher chakras are not yet activated.

The pendulum is an instrument that can receive pulses through the energy body. Your body is a conduit that channels pranic flow. The better shape your body is in, the better the conduit for the energy flow. Some people are natural conduits of energy. There is energy flowing in their being. They are high energy, motivated and enthusiastic. These attitudes represent a strong and balanced energy flow in the chakra system. The pendulum can move swiftly and easily on the pranic current.

If one has a strong energy practice, their body is in the habit of energizing itself. An energized body has more energy flowing through it. The stronger the flow of energy, the stronger the current of energy that can flow through your form.

If you come to this divination practice understanding energy flow and energy healing, you will have an easier time working with the pendulum. Lack of energy, or blocked energy channels, in general, will block one's ability to move the instrument. Starting an energy exercise like yoga, Tai Chi or Qi Gong is highly recommended. You can use your intention to make other types of exercises, like running or being on the elliptical machine, an energy body practice.

Finally, it might not be time for you to practice pendulum work. In many ways, the practice calls to you and you know that it is something that you should do. There is a strong desire to contact your angelic team and it's encouraging when there is an exchange of information. If you have a strong desire to learn, but can't make the pendulum move yet, consider changing the focus of your work to self-healing and purification of the chakra system which is a prior step to divination work and working with your angelic team.

Chapter 2. Pendulum Precautions

Is Working with the Pendulum Dangerous?

A client came in and asked the question, "What's the difference between using an Ouija Board and a pendulum?" The Ouija Board is a mediumship tool for connecting with the spirit realm similar to a pendulum. There are three differences. The first difference is the "intention" and the knowingness of where the divination material originated from. In the case of the Ouija Board, its origins are in dark magic and indeed there are very conscious negative energies, or lost souls that are very easy to channel, that will communicate through it.

This work originates from the Light Realms, which is known as Heaven in the traditional Christian religion. This work is ordained and blessed by the Ascended White Light Masters and the white light of Divine Source.

The second difference is your personal intention. Your strong intentions about what you are attempting to channel make a difference. "Spiritual confidence" is a term I use to express the correct attitude when approaching divination work. You need to feel confident that you are working with your angelic team. You need to clearly articulate your attunement to a representative of Divine Source; this would be an Ascended Master. Finally you need to have a strong and steady spiritual practice that works for you. Those three elements produce a faith, trust and confidence that you need to approach the invisible spirit realm.

I was very naive when I started to do the work of asking the pendulum questions. I had a strong knowingness that I was attuned to love and light and everything was coming from a place of light. This "spiritual confidence" came from my steady yoga practice and a devotional attitude. I was practicing under the watchful gaze of Yogananda, Jesus Christ and Babaji Krishna while I was practicing yoga at the Ananda Community in Seattle. I knew I was a devotee and I knew I was protected and everything was coming from a place of goodness and light.

The third difference is the 3 pendulum languages are designed to work with your angelic team for the purposes of spiritual growth and assisting you in your healing practice. The intention is very clear and your white light guides will know the intention of your heart. In the case of those that use the Ouija Board their intentions are unclear. The divination tool is used for entertainment, general curiosity or for the purpose of contacting lost souls and dark energies.

"Spiritual bypassing" is a term I use to describe a person that gets into divination work without developing correct spiritual attitudes or attunements to the white light. Some people are born psychic. You can be psychic and not spiritual. There are many gifted people with psychic abilities that develop different "siddhi". Siddhi is a yogic Sanskrit word that means yogic powers. These are spiritual powers and psychic gifts that are attained through spiritual advancement. These yogic powers are granted by the guides so the candidate can support their mission in the world.

There are many yogic texts that warn against developing yogic powers without being under the watchful gaze of a yogic master or Ascended Master. You can be psychic and not spiritually attuned to the white light. This book is focused on contacting your angelic team to be a healer or helper in the world. And of course, there is our modern day story of this principle in the Star Wars series. Anakin Skywalker was developing to be a Jedi, a spiritual warrior for the force of good and justice, unfortunately, he was swayed by the power of the dark.

The pendulum can draw to it both white light energies and neutral or dark energies. It can be dangerous if you are not clear about your intentions and what you would like to receive by practicing this deeply spiritual work.

How I Developed Spiritual Confidence

In my late twenties I lived in Seattle, Washington and practiced yoga at the Ananda Community. Living in an intentional Christ Conscious community was amazing. I found joy in meditation. After completing my bachelors and going to work for a corporation, in the evenings I started to study Raja yoga, which means royal yoga and includes many different yoga techniques.

I was practicing daily and completely immersed on the path. At the same time, I was also open-minded and working at a new age bookstore. I was exploring many diverse ideas from world religions, divination tools, hypnosis, channeling and past life regression. I was also studying working with the Archangels, spirit guides and shamanic journeys. One day, I started playing with the pendulum and it moved very easily. I was really excited about this. I was just certain it was my angels trying to communicate with me.

Like many people, I picked up the pendulum and played with it a bit, but I didn't really understand how to use it. I played with the pendulum over the next few years. During these early years, I was using the pendulum to ask Yes/No questions every time my life hit a difficult transition and felt I needed guidance. But I didn't practice often, and I really didn't understand how to heal with it.

It wasn't until eight years later after I completed my graduate degree in Western psychology that I picked up the pendulum again. I had resumed teaching yoga. I was feeling good about my life and my spiritual path. I was full of spiritual confidence.

From my perspective the pendulum wasn't dangerous at all. It was a make-shift telephone that allowed me to speak to the spirit guides and I felt it was really assisting me in my healing work. But I did notice, about two years into the practice of using the pendulum daily for spirit communication, that on occasion I would get interference. I also learned about negative energies and the need to clear myself and clear my office space.

Ascension Evolution

There is nothing more exciting than once you start to ascend. Ascension is a term that describes human spiritual evolution. Ascension is the process where one starts to experience the astral or angelic dimensions. Another way to express this is one starts to have 5th dimension experiences.

We are living in the 3rd dimension in the physical universe. If you are interested in this work you are in or approaching the 4th dimension, which is somewhere in-between the 3rd and 5th dimension. If you are reading this, you are in the ascension process and evolving to the 5th dimension. More information on this topic can be found in my book **The 10 Cosmic Dimensions, A Spiritual Guidebook to Ascension**.

Many lightworkers are able to bridge the two dimensions. Countless people have reported to me about seeing angels, orbs, lost souls, dark entities, galactics (with both positive and negative motivation) and other 5th dimensional elements. If you are one of these people, then you know without a doubt that there are other dimensions existing and operating in and around our 3rd dimension physical universe.

Sometimes people come into my office and say something like, "I don't know what I believe. I know there's a higher power, but I don't know if I believe in angels or negative energy or if there is a heaven or not". From my perspective, of course there are angels, they have assisted me in writing these books. I know I am not moving the pendulum. I know when there is interference with my channeling work.

Yes there were definitely angels and spirit guides and now I was finding there was also negative energy. People would come in feeling heavy and hearing a voice that told them they were worthless. The next week they would report the voice was gone. I became aware of 3rd party negative energy and that it was a separate consciousness, nestled in one of the seven chakras. It was parasitic, and once it released the client reported feeling lighter and the symptoms subsided.

Firsthand experience is your best teacher. If the pendulum moves for you, you have started to investigate the mysteries of the unseen realms. There is no need to convince you because you have practical experience. The ascension process is the ability to spiritually evolve to have these experiences. Ascension is exciting. It's an amazing experience when you start to perceive the world and our reality from a different perspective.

Interference

Yes, there is such a thing as "interference". Interference is when you are trying to contact your angelic team, and negative energy, which is in the same space, starts to interfere with your ability to channel and communicate clearly with your spirit team.

One of the advantages of the pendulum is that it is an easy way to communicate with your angelic team. One of the disadvantages is that it is an easy tool to receive interference. Remember using the pendulum is training wheels for developing clairaudience, the ability to hear your guides. Clairaudience is a direct connection, the ability for a negative energy to interfere is little to none.

The pendulum is a tool. There are a few ways in which negative energy can interfere. Negative energy can be in the location of the space, especially if you share a space with other people not on a spiritual path. There could be negative energy within you, or in another person.

If you start to get bad answers, or the answers don't match your intuitive knowledge about the situation, it's likely you are experiencing some type of interference. One thing I learned in the early stages of my work was that I could always ask the question, "Is this a negative energy?" and oftentimes the pendulum would spin, yes. I didn't panic or become fearful. I simply understood that there was some debris in the area that needed to be cleared first.

My guides taught me this universal principle when using the pendulum. The instrument will not lie when you ask for the identity of the entity giving you the information. If you are speaking with a lost soul or a negative energy, the pendulum will tell you.

As we learn the languages of pendulum communication for spirit contact, there is a protocol for asking questions to assist you if you feel you are experiencing interference. This topic brings us back to the question, "Is the pendulum a dangerous tool?" This is where spiritual confidence and your calling as a healer come into play. You have to feel very certain that your angels are with you and momentary inference will pass after a brief meditation.

Also in the **100 Chakra System** book, I discuss that negative energy has different strengths, which I measure on a scale from 10 to 100+ degrees. Even a small negative energy that is 40 degrees is enough to cause a potential interference. Which bring us to the next question in the protocol, "Am I clear enough to channel?" Clearing is the process of removing negative energies from your outer auric field, the 100 chakras, and your environment. It is important that your space feels clear and you feel emotionally balanced. In general a 10 minute clearing exercise and 20 minutes of mediation will prepare you for Divine communication.

Hear the call. Our world is overwhelmed with negative energy. It is a fact of our modern world and over-populated societal structure. Angels and spirit guides want to work with you. The Divine white light forces need all the lightworkers like never before. Develop spiritual confidence and perform divination with the intention of connecting to your angelic team without fear. Remember, your light and your angels are always stronger than any darkness that might dwell in the world.

Protocol for Using the Pendulum

Over the years I developed a protocol for avoiding potential interference. Before you start to channel your angelic team, first follow this suggested protocol.

It is best to have a sacred space or altar in your home for clearing and meditation. Approach your space with an attitude of devotion and service to communicate. Seek to commune with the Light Realms and your assigned angelic team. Sit for at least 10 minutes and ask your angelic team to clear your energy body from the experiences of the day, then meditate for 10 minutes.

There are a number of clearing exercises you can do. You can do a few rounds of simple kriya breaths. You can listen to a guided meditation to clear your chakras. You can put your hand on your chakras and direct energy flow where you need it. Some people will use crystals or essential oils to clear. You can also learn to clear with the pendulum which is discussed in the next book in this series.

After clearing and meditation ask the pendulum the following questions:

- **Am I clear enough to channel?**
  (Confirm you have done enough clearing work)

- **Is this a negative energy?**
  (Ask about who you are communicating with)

- **Am I a female? Is my name Jane?**
  (Ask a question you know the answer to)

- **Should I jump off a bridge?**
  (Ask a stupid question you know the answer to)

These questions validate the source of the entity you are contacting and allow you to feel confident you are channeling your angelic team.

Ideally, before you work with any divination tool, you should make sure that your chakra system is balanced. The first question is, "Am I clear enough to channel?" Many of us have such busy lives that we forget what it feels like when the 7 Primary Chakras are clear and balanced. In my practice, I ask people to notice how they feel after an energy healing session. Most people walk in the room with uncomfortable emotions. They have been uncomfortable for so long that they don't even know what balanced feels like.

Other people with a yoga or energy healing practice know what it feels like when they are balanced. For example, lightworkers that practice hatha yoga know they feel more balanced after yoga than when they walked in the door. If you are scratching your head and wondering if you have ever been balanced, then find an energy healer and experience the difference between the before and after feeling. You are also invited to clear and meditate using the self-healing meditations found on my YouTube channel. 'Search Raven Shamballa Clearing Meditations'.

If you ask the question, "Am I clear enough to channel?" and the answer is a "no", then ask, "How long should I clear for?" Time mark questions are covered in the next section. If you receive the answer "15 minutes", then stop and continue to clear. If you ask this question and get a "yes", don't stop there. Keep going with the validation questions. I have learned you often have to ask a few questions to make sure.

Assuming you are clear enough to channel, next find out who you are working with. Ask the question "Is this a negative energy?" If you get a "yes", don't get upset. Just relax and clear for another 10 minutes. If you are curious, you can use your pendulum to ask, "Is this a negative energy, a lost soul, or something else?"

Our world is cluttered with energy debris and lost soul fragments. Many lightworkers are empaths and pick up energy all day long, some of that energy may be lost soul fragments. Early on in my energy healing practice I learned that lost souls often attach to lightworkers. Many advanced souls are tasked with the extracurricular activity of helping to cross lost souls over to the Light Realms. If you receive the answer, your communicating with a lost soul or negative energy, don't panic. Ask your clearing angels to help you. They will assist the energy to cross over to the other side. If you get the answer the communication is from a negative energy, again, no big deal, just continue to clear for 10 minutes and ask again.

Next ask a question you know the answer to and then ask a stupid question. In both cases if you get the wrong answer on the pendulum then you know you are not quite clear enough to channel. If you get all the validating questions correct you are clear enough to channel without interference.

When I first started doing the channeling work, I didn't get interference. I went my first two years using the instrument and was confident I was connected to my Higherself and my angelic team. As time went on and my line of questioning became more advanced, I noticed interference. My angels told me I should be honored, I was advancing in dimensional consciousness. I was receiving challenges to my work of pulling negative energy out of people. Like all jedi knights that advance on the cosmic consciousness scale there is testing that may come. As lightworkers we remember, "No Fear, The Light is Always Victorious over the Dark." As you grow in psychic development you may be tested along the way. Remember to use your common sense, if the answer doesn't feel right to you, immediately ask "Is this a negative energy?" The pendulum will not lie to you.

The other information that my angels gave me was to please remember that communicating with the Divine and its representatives is sacred and deeply spiritual work. In other times in our history, channeling the heavens would not even be approached without living in a monastery surrounded by purified beings in a location where the signature of the energy field was bright light. A master teacher would be nearby and the student would be hand-selected to learn the spiritual work.

In this day and age, that is not the case. What was once sacred knowledge and passed through verbal tradition is now spattered here and there all over the internet. When I had my first psychic opening, the guide at the time told me, "You think you know something, but really you don't know anything. Everything you have ever learned was only read about or learned in a weekend workshop."

We practice this sacred exchange in our apartments and homes in very filthy and dirty modern cities. Many of us have family members that are not healthy and even radiate with negative energy. If you live in a large metropolitan area, don't be surprised if you get interference, don't take it personally and don't be afraid. Keep working to clear your space and clear your energy body.

This is one of the reasons why the Ascended Masters started to incarnate advanced souls onto Earth, who are not on the wheel of karma. They are born clear up to the 100th chakra and it's easier for these advanced souls to connect at higher dimensions and perform healing work and divination work. If you are interested in this work, you are most likely an advanced soul and desire a direct communication with your angelic team.

Chapter 3.   Pendulum Basics

How to Hold the Pendulum

There are two basic ways to hold the pendulum. The traditional way is to hold the pendulum from the weight at the top of the string. In this case the string is very long and the pendulum makes long and slow swing movements. This hold is good for beginners or to see if you can get the pendulum to swing. If you have never tried to move the pendulum then start with the long grip hold. It will take longer for the pendulum to swing, but you can easily see the movement. The long grip hold is traditionally taught when people use the pendulum charts.

Once you can get the pendulum to move, change from the long grip hold to the short grip hold. The short grip hold allows the pendulum to move faster. For the pendulum on the hand language the short grip hold is definitely recommended. For both the long grip and short grip hold, use your dominant hand to hold the string. For most of us, that is the right hand, so in this work I will refer to the dominant hand as the right hand.

With a short hold you want to pinch the string with the right hand 1 or 2 inches above the pendulum. When we are practicing the pendulum language on the hand, some practitioners might feel most comfortable with a 1 inch hold. The short hold allows for quick and precise movements of the instrument on the flat surface of your left palm.

If your pendulum has a long string, cord or chain, feel free to cut it. Most cords are very easy to snip with scissors. You can also gather the remaining string with the palm of your right hand. Most people find that holding the remaining string is awkward. Whether you are working the pendulum on your hand or using a chart, the short hold is fastest and most accurate to report answers. For demonstrations on how to hold the pendulum, see my YouTube videos, search 'Raven Shamballa Pendulum'.

The tip of the pendulum is important. Make sure that the tip is like a ball point pen. With the medal pendulums this is quite easy to see. At the beginning

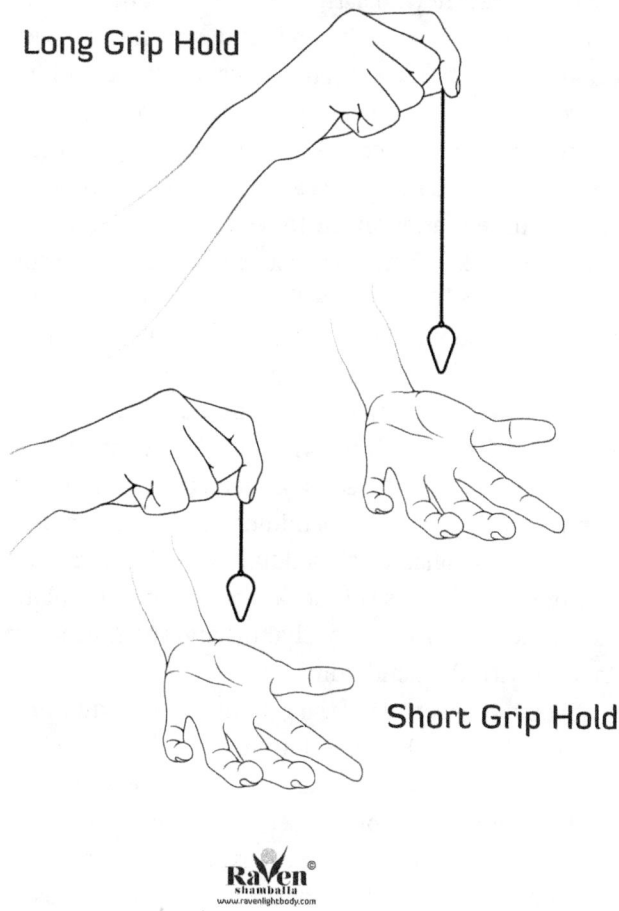

HOW TO HOLD THE PENDULUM

Long Grip Hold

Short Grip Hold

some students find it difficult to get the pendulum to move. When you first begin, only the tip of the pendulum may move. When you are using a chart the tip will go to the specific location. If the pendulum is a heavy weight or doesn't have a well-defined tip it is hard to get an accurate reading. As you advance, and you can make the pendulum move easily, the tip point is less important.

What Type of Pendulum Should I Use?

Over the years people have asked me what type of pendulum to purchase and does it matter. Another question I get is, if I purchase a crystal pendulum does it matter what crystal I buy? The answer to both of these questions is it doesn't really matter what type of pendulum you purchase. Once you get good at moving the instrument you can make your car key swing by holding an ornament and letting it dangle. Anything will swing, once you know how to activate the pendulum.

If you are new to moving the pendulum and it moves for you, but just barely, then a heavy metal pendulum is recommended. The heavier the pendulum the easier it is to move. In this course, we are "reading with the pendulum". That means we are asking questions with the instrument and waiting to see the answer.

In this work, I distinguish between "reading with the pendulum" and "clearing with the pendulum". Clearing with the pendulum refers to the practice of chakra balancing. In this case, the pendulum should be lighter, like a crystal pendulum or plastic bead pendulum. This is because the pendulum swings faster during chakra balancing and for this reason a metal pendulum is too heavy. Clearing with the pendulum will be covered in another book called **Chakra Balancing with the Pendulum** which follows this book. That book will explain how to clear the 7 Primary Chakras and the Ascending Chakras with the pendulum.

If you have been using the pendulum for a while and can definitely get the pendulum to move, then you can use a lighter pendulum like a crystal or plastic bead pendulum. In general, ornate decorations are not recommended. For example smaller beads glued onto the crystal pendulum, or the string of the pendulum has beads or crystals attached to decorate it. When you activate your energy body and the current is strong and steady, the pendulum will move rather fast. Glued on extras for decoration can end up being a hindrance, especially when you use the short-hold grip.

One thing to keep in mind if you purchase a crystal pendulum: the crystal needs to be cleared. Crystals are like an energy source, they wear out and need to be recharged. I have had crystals break or fall out if I use them too long without clearing. If you have a strong energy practice like Reiki or Kundalini yoga, you can most likely clear the crystals with your hand. Crystals can also be cleared with salty water, or by recharging them in sunlight or moonlight. It is recommended that you clear the pendulum after each use. If that feels bothersome to you, you can use a plastic or metal pendulum.

On occasion I will get feedback from students that their crystal pendulum broke. In this case the crystal was very dirty with energy and is overwhelmed and then breaks. Crystals have magical properties and require extra care. Take this into consideration when deciding to purchase a crystal pendulum.

In this work, your angelic team is giving you the answers to your questions. The pendulum is simply a tool for communication. The crystal and the magical properties of the crystal pendulum don't have much to do with the movement of the swing. In this practice, the crystal pendulum is just a tool to show the swing of the movement and receive a communication from your guidance team. The type of crystal doesn't really matter, so purchase your favorite crystal, just keep in mind that if the crystal gets too full of energy or gets dirty it could break.

TYPES OF PENDULUMS

Metal and Crystal Pendulums

What if I Have Programed My Pendulum in a Different Way?

In this book, I am sharing with you information I have learned over the years working with my angelic team. If you have been working with the pendulum on your own and you have programed your pendulum to mean different things, that is absolutely fine. Go with the language that you and your guides have developed.

One time I was working with a client and she said that her pendulum swung counter-clockwise for "yes". I asked her angelic team about this, and indeed, they had already set the program language and didn't want it changed. There is no need to make changes to your programming, just modify the information in a way that suits you and your angelic team.

Chapter 4. Contacting your Angelic Team

Create a Sacred Space

Communicating with the Divine is a great honor. If you can naturally move the pendulum without any effort, you are most likely an advanced lightworker and have found this work to assist you with direct communication with your angelic team. The purpose of the direct link is to assist you in your healing work and your mission on Earth.

As you approach the pendulum practice keep these points in mind. Be respectful of the angels, guides and Ascended Masters that will accompany you on your journey. Before the modern age, a candidate wanting to learn the art of Divine communication would be selected from spiritual elders or chosen from birth, or groomed through diligent spiritual practice before being selected to learn the practice.

If you were fortunate to have a guru in your local community you wanted to learn from, you would approach the teacher with reverence and respect for the Divine. You would most likely be advanced on your path and strong in your meditations and spiritual practices. The guru may ask you to practice a specific way before feeling you were qualified to learn the sacred practices.

Practice would take place in a sacred location, perhaps in a monastery or temple, or a place that was considered sacred and purified. The area would be clear and intended for Divine union. There may be rituals, chanting and sacred prayers said before trying to commune. There would be no chance of negative energy anywhere in the location or in your person, or people around you, as there would be an abundance of Divine light. Like-minded people would assist you in holding the light.

In our world, it can be hard to come by sacred spaces, especially if you feel put off by formal religious paths. We have to create a sacred space in our living area. Many people create sacred spaces in small rooms or closets. If you don't have much space, create an altar.

An altar is a table or dedicated space for your spiritual practice. You can place meaningful spiritual items on your altar. You can also place selenite crystals around your room or altar to help clear and purify the space. If you share a room or have a small space that will not accommodate an altar, then create a dedicated spiritual box and place all of your spiritual tools in the Divine box. More information on creating a sacred space is given in Chapter 6 in the section, "3 Pendulum Charts for Meeting Your Angelic Team".

- Use common sense in asking questions.
- Don't ask the same questions over and over.
- If you are overly emotional and confused, consult a reader.
- Avoid questions about someone else's friend or family (for example, your client is asking you to channel information about their best friend's failing marriage).
- Avoid gossipy questions.
- Avoid questions that come from a place of fear.

Guidelines for Asking Pendulum Questions

Guidelines for Giving a Pendulum Reading

- Make sure you have permission to read someone.

- If you feel you have information for someone, ask them if they would like to receive it first before sharing the information.

- Make sure you speak with spiritual confidence about whom you are attuned to and who is giving you this information.

- Avoid the concept of fortune teller, rather you are helping yourself or a client to discover potentials and possibilities.

The Line of Questioning

I have found that the type of questions you ask and the way in which you ask the questions are important. This book is evidence that the veils are lifting. Humans are no longer cut off from higher dimensions. The reference to the "veils lifting" comes from yoga philosophy. The veil is a boundary that prevents us from comprehending and communing with the Divine in other dimensions.

'Maya' is a yogic word that means 'illusion'. 'Maya' references our temporary Earth experience and our limited perspective from the human vantage point. Advanced souls hold very high ranks in the astral realm. Part of the game of life on Earth is being born with amnesia. The trick is to remember who you are, and awaken as soon as possible. Once lightworkers remember who they are and why they came to Earth, they stop feeling sorry for themselves for being born on such a low frequency planet, we get over it and get to work! You are supposed to be here!

As the veil is lifted we gain access to the other side. But my experience working with guides is that they may not want to give it all away. Often people come to the practice with the attitude, "please just tell me, what the guides want me to do?" One may feel lost and not yet know their true purpose.

Even though you can start a conversation and build a relationship with your angelic team, you may not get all the answers you desire right up front. The guides may not want to give away the ending to the story. The guides are watching in real time, different processes and potentials as they unfold in our time stream.

We are co-creating with our angelic teams in real time. We are co-creating with every decision we make and every intention we put out to the universe. The guides want to work with you, listen to you and help to create energy and enthusiasm for a great work to do good in the world. They also want you to grow and learn. The spirit guides see value in having you make discoveries along the way.

Take for example the question, "Will I get the job I just interviewed for?" The answer could depend on a multitude of factors. Rather than a yes or a no, you might receive the answer - counter-clockwise spin, which means, "I am not ready to tell you yet, or there is not enough information to answer your question."

The guides may not yet know the answers you seek. There are other people interviewing for the position. The interviewers have their own preferences. It might be your dream job, but you are quite unaware of the people that work there and if the vibration is right for your growth or your ability to mentor others. A better way to ask the questions, would be a probability question. For example, "Is this potential opportunity 50% likely or unlikely?", "Should I continue to be persistent or should I be non-attached?", "On a scale from 1-6, 6 being the best, how would my guides scale this environment for me?"

After you receive the answers, rest in faith. Put the pendulum down. Have no fear. Cultivate faith and trust and move forward knowing that because you are aligned to the light, everything will work out for your greatest good and highest happiness.

Questions to Avoid

There are a few questions that you want to avoid when you start to communicate with your angelic team. Here is what I learned over the years: The guides still want you to use your common sense, and in many cases you might be the expert who knows best. For example, we can start to ask too many detailed questions. "What is the best design for this project?", "What kind of marketing plan would be the best to sell my products?" or "Should I purchase all these tools, if so how many and what kind?"

Guides want to provide guidance, but they don't want to be in the role of personal assistant or just defaulting to get all your answers. They want you to make your own daily decisions.

They want you to make choices about personal preferences. The guides want you to decorate and spend according to your desires. They want you to check in with them, but it's not necessary for every detailed question. Use your discernment, there is balance in every spiritual practice.

Avoid asking the same questions over and over. If you start to get inconsistent answers the guides may be trying to tell you, "We already answered that question, stop asking." I remember there have been times in my journey when my guides felt I was asking too many questions. Or I was asking questions I already knew the answers to. Although patient, the guides can become quiet if they feel you already know that answers and more likely, if you just don't like the answer the guides are giving you.

If the answer doesn't make sense, or it feels off to you intuitively, then go with your gut internal guidance. For example, imagine you are asking the guides if you should go to a workshop. The pendulum may swing "yes" and a scaling question may reveal that the workshop is 5 out of 6 (6 means you should definitely attend). Your guides are all for it. But you know financially that the cost doesn't make sense right now.

In this case, use common sense. Yes, your angels may want you to go, but the timing could be off. If the guides really want you to go to the workshop, the money will manifest. Think outside of the box. Ideas will come to you. At the end of the day, you have to go with your common sense and your gut feeling. Sometimes the guides will ask you to take leaps of faith, but you have to balance that with your free will and life experience. In order to make decisions, use the antenna on your Heart Chakra. If your heart feels joyful and excited, do that! If you are lackluster or feel low energy, or are not sure, don't do that.

If you still feel confused or are overly emotional about a situation, consult a psychic reader rather than your pendulum. Emotions are very confusing and change rapidly. Transitions are quite difficult and cause emotional imbalance. Often times we tell the universe what we want, and then when change happens we can become overwhelmed and scared. Strong emotions mean the chakra system is fluctuating. The pendulum may misread your changing and confused emotions. Seek a counselor that is neutral, grounded and not attached to the outcome of the situation.

When you ask questions, it is appropriate to ask about yourself or someone you know personally, but avoid asking questions about someone else's friends and family. For example, you might ask if your cousin needs support, or how they are doing. But you would not want to start asking questions about your cousin's friend. For example, "Is their friend the reason why your cousin is in so much pain? Did the friend do something bad and make this event happen?"

From the perspective of the guides, they may not know the answer because they are not the guides for the person you ask about. They are in observation of you and your story, not everyone else's story. Also it's none of your business. The person is too far removed from your inner sphere. This question doesn't really have to do with your personal growth. If you are asking for your cousin, the question should be focused on their journey and not on the cousin's friend's journey.

Avoid asking gossipy or fear-based questions. This practice assumes you are at a certain level of integrity and spiritual maturity. Avoid questions in which you are trying to find out about rumors. For example, "I heard Jack is having an affair with Sara? Yes or No?" The guides will roll their eyes at this question.

These types of questions are not focused on spiritual growth, healing work or guidance for your mission. If you are in the habit of asking these kinds of questions and regularly get answers you believe are true, you may be consulting a lost soul, a departed family member or a negative energy. Ask some validation questions and confirm who you are speaking with.

Finally, avoid asking questions that come from a place of fear, or hold fear-based attitudes. For example, "If I lose my job, what will happen to me? How long might I be unemployed?", "Will this person die soon?", "If I take this risk, will I fail?" These questions are not appropriate because they come from a place of fear and worry. The guides will not entertain questions with these attitudes. More appropriate questions are, "Has this job served its purpose, is it time for me to transition?", "Is this a good time to consult a dying family member, am I emotionally strong enough to take these roles and responsibilities?"

Over the years I have consulted with my angelic team, and I have also consulted with clients guides. What I have found is the guides have individual and unique personalities. Some are playful and patient, others are rigid and stern. In many cases, they have known you for lifetimes. They may even be a good friend to you on the other side. They understand your mission and potential. They also understand you are in limited human consciousness. They want to communicate with you. Just remember to be respectful in the way you approach your practice and the line of questions you ask.

Giving a Reading with the Pendulum

Advanced lightworkers who become good at using the pendulum naturally gravitate to wanting to give psychic readings to friends or clients. Here are some guidelines for giving a pendulum reading. Make sure you have permission to read someone before you ask questions of the guides. Also, if you feel you have information for someone, ask them if they would like to receive it first before sharing the information. Not everyone wants to know the answer, or will be open-minded about what you have to say.

Make sure you can speak with spiritual confidence about who you are, who you are channeling and where your information is coming from. Make sure to tell them the purpose of the reading is for their greatest good and highest happiness.

Avoid pendulum work in front of a client. The primary reason for this is a client's auric field and chakras are dirty and you could experience interference that is originating with them. You may want to do clearing work with a client, prior to reading the pendulum in front of them if this is your practice. Of course, if you feel you are advanced and have strong spiritual confidence, you can use your own guidance to know if you should work with the pendulum in front of others. For beginners to the practice, it is not suggested.

Avoid the concept that you are a fortune teller and you can tell someone their future.

While many psychics can receive information or visions about the future that are accurate, they are not set in stone, they are potentials and probabilities. Even my guides caution against the idea of "telling the future." Our reality is making itself up in real time. There are many factors that are hard to account for. There are changes we didn't see coming. Other people have their own free will and choice. Sometimes we are assigned to meet someone and they "go left". I refer to this term to mean, instead of the person being on path, they get distracted or a malicious vice comes in and the person goes off path, to the left. It's easy to go off path in our confusing world.

Rather than telling the future, look for potentials and probabilities. Probability questions ask, "Is this 50% likely to occur or not occur?". If the event is likely to occur, then you should relax and allow the process of your life to unfold. If it is not likely to occur, you should be non-attached to the outcome and see what manifests. Guidance is giving clues as to the appropriate direction but we still have to move through the experience of not knowing and having faith that everything is going to turn out positive and ultimately for our greatest good.

In some cases you may want to ask questions about family and friends that you believe would be in their highest best interest. You might feel like they will not be receptive to your psychic work and therefore it might be hard for you to ask for permission. For example, imagine that your mom was dealing with health issues and you wanted to ask your guides, "Are there any health and healing products that I should recommend to my mom?" The question arises, "Would it be okay to receive this information and then give it to my mom without asking her permission?"

In this case, ask your guides. They will tell you directly. Usually, if you have someone's highest, best interest at heart, they will give you information to pass to a loved one. If your angelic team feels that the question is inappropriate, they will give you a counter-clockwise answer which means, "None of Your Business" or the pendulum will halt to still point meaning, "No comment", or "Not Willing to Answer You". These commands are explained in Chapter 7, Pendulum on the Hand.

As you build your relationship with your angelic team and learn how to ask questions, keep asking your guides if it is appropriate for you to be a psychic reader to others. The guides will be very direct with their answer. You may get an enthusiastic "Definitely!" answer, or you may get the answer, "No", "Not Yet". If you hold the intention that you want to be a reader that uses the pendulum, your guides will work to develop you so that you can give readings. If you are concerned that you don't have permission or if you're not ready to be a psychic reader, simply ask your guidance team. They will be very direct with you.

Humans and Guides Have Different Perspectives

Here is another point to remember when working with the pendulum. There are times when we don't like what our guides have to say. We are dealing with fear of change and self-esteem and it is hard to make the changes we need to make to progress us along our spiritual path.

People will come in for a reading and ask me what their guides think about ending an unhappy relationship. The guides may answer, "Yes" on the first session, end the relationship. As a counselor you might remark, "Follow your heart, your heart is not happy. The guides are encouraging you to make a change." The client then goes on to present several reasons as to why this is not possible. As a counselor, I just listen. I have watched "guides" allow their "candidates" to move through their own process, even when they have given clear guidance months or years before. The guides wait for the candidate to be ready to change. Most of us know what to do; we are just frightened to make the change.

Here is another difference in perspective. While humans are very concerned with issues of money, love and career advancement, the spirit guides have different motivation for your path. Guides are concerned with your spiritual mission and with healing and helping the world. The priorities are different but the guides have a different perspective on life after death and one's mission relative to the short earthly timeline.

From a human perspective our main concern might be, "How am I going to pay off my debt?" From a guide perspective they are considering, "What is the best placement for personal growth, fulfillment and service to others?" Remember that most of the lightworkers are volunteers and most are **not** on the wheel of karma. Lightworkers are not incarnated to "learn life's lessons" to get off the repetitive wheel. Lightworkers are here for mission and for service work in the dark world. We are deployed to this planet with every guarantee for returning to the Light Realm after our missions are completed. For more information on the concept of the volunteers, read the **10 Cosmic Dimensions, A Spiritual Guidebook to Ascension**.

The spirit guides were with you prior to the time you incarnated. At that time, the advanced souls created Divine missions. Those missions are the most important reasons why you chose to volunteer on such a difficult planet. While humans are thinking about money, love and children, the guides are thinking about life purpose. What's the best placement for you to fulfill your mission? Guides will answer questions about love and money, of course, it's just they are more focused on assisting the advanced soul with their missions. Guides prefer communication to be focused on healing work or understanding how to better help other people.

The pendulum is an amazing tool. Ask for guidance and be willing to accept the answers. Remember, especially for the beginner, you will have better success and less interference if you ask questions regarding health, healing and advancing spiritually in the direction of your life purpose.

Remember, use your intuition about a situation. If you are asking questions and start to get answers that feel off to you, go back to the validation questions. Confirm whom you are communicating with. If the answer feels off to you then it probably is, or if you give readings and you know it's not a typical answer, ask more questions. Don't be afraid to ask more questions until you feel satisfied with the guide's response.

Chapter 5. More Information on Your Angelic Team

How I Met My Angelic Team

During graduate school I returned home to help pay for the high cost of college. I was sad to leave Seattle, Washington, which had a strong yoga community. I returned to the orchards and rural area of Central California. Gone were the days when there were plenty of yoga teachers and spiritualists to find. I returned home to a conservative community with more experience in these areas. I was without a local mentor. I really wanted to contact my angelic team directly for guidance.

At this time, I had read several books on channeling and could do automatic writing and receive angel messages. I was searching for direction and flipping angel divination cards almost daily. I was playing with the pendulum and asking Yes/No questions. One day I picked up a book about angels and became curious about my angelic team. I wondered how many angels were on my team. I decided to ask my pendulum with the number chart. "How many angels are on my team?" The answer I got at the time was fifteen.

Next, I wanted to know my angel's names. I remembered the alphabet chart. I could use the pendulum, but the swing of the pendulum was slow at the time. I remember feeling like it took a long time to gather the letters, so I wanted to know how many letters were in the name. I went back to the number chart. The answer returned: there were twelve letters in the angel's name. I used the pendulum to learn the name Kundalini Ray. Then I wanted to know if the angel was a male or female. I got female. I was really excited.

The next evening, I was interested in trying to speak with Kundalini Ray. I asked her to come forward. I wanted to know what she helped me with. Without being clairaudient you can't really ask 'how' or 'why' questions, so I went back to the pendulum charts. I asked, "What is a word that describes how you help me, how many letters?" I got four. I went back to the alphabet chart. The pendulum swing was Y – O – G – A. She helped me with my yoga teaching practice.

Later that week, I was teaching a private yoga class with three clients. We were in a small office and we went through our regular hatha yoga routine. Then we went into Shavasana, corpse pose, which is the deep relaxation pose you lie in after the physical practice. As I led the relaxation, I felt a wonderful energy. The words of the meditation came easily to me. I felt supported with soulful words coming from an intuitive place. After class, all three clients were profoundly affected. One client said she heard angel wings. We were all deeply moved by the meditation.

When I got home, I went straight to my altar. Maybe I was channeling Kundalini Ray? So I meditated a few minutes, picked up the pendulum to ask, "Were you with me? Was I channeling you?" To that question, the answer came, "Yes." Then I heard a message intuitively, "I am here to assist you with your yoga practice." Then I asked, "Do you help me with other things?" She answered, "No." Then I remembered that I had fifteen angels. "Do all the angels have specialties?" The reply was, "Yes." Finally, I asked, "How long have you been in my auric field?" I got the number eighteen. That made sense to me. I started my yoga practice at eighteen years old.

This event happened about fifteen years ago, I was in my early thirties. My psychic skills were in development. I was at a novice level. I was only asking Yes/No questions and using the Number and Alphabet Chart. It was painstaking and time-consuming to channel in all the information, but I figured it out. I learned all fifteen of my angel's names, and I channeled in all the ways in which they were assigned to assist me.

At times I would attempt automatic writing and it was hit or miss. Sometimes I would get a message or a paragraph, other times nothing.

Automatic writing is the writing exercise in which you channel Divine representatives.

You sit down with pen and paper, or in front of a keyboard and quiet your mind. You intend to receive a message. Then you meditate and wait for words to come forward on the page. In this way, I was trying to make contact. If I received a message, I would use the pendulum to ask, "Who sent this message?" I was also using the pendulum on my hand. I assigned each finger an angel name. In this way I understood the different voices coming from my team.

Not long after that, I received a beautiful message. It was a page of automatic writing; it was fluid, positive and encouraging. The message itself was not any new information, but I felt my being was elevated, like I was on a higher frequency when I wrote it. When I came out of meditation, I looked over the writing. It felt more sophisticated to me than other messages. Who sent this message to me? I went to the pendulum on my hand and got counter-clockwise.

Was this energy different than an angel? I got, "Yes". I went back to the alphabet chart. "How many letters in the word?" I got five. I channeled it in, G -U-I-D- E. I had received the message from a guide, a spirit guide. How many guides did I have? At that time, I got the number ten. I channeled in the name of the one who sent the message. It was Zucoluxowl. He confirmed that was the name and he was male. I asked him, "Would you mind if I give you a nickname?" He said no, and I decided to call him Zuc.

And that was the beginning of my journey contacting my spirit guides and asking them questions about yoga, divination work, chakra balancing, the workshops I should take and other questions I had in relationship to my spiritual practices. The time period was early 2000s. Facebook did not exist, and the internet was in its infancy. Google was not yet commercialized and the general public didn't have easy access to creating websites.

Since I had no 3rd dimensional teachers in my local area, and no internet at the time, I relied heavily on the pendulum and Yes/No questions to guide me and teach me in the healing arts. I was thrilled I had such a communication link. As time passed I was introduced to more angels and spirit guides. When channeling with the pendulum, I got in the habit of asking, "Are you an angel, or are you a spirit guide?"

The Difference between Angels and Guides

The questioning continued. I was so curious. I wanted to know how many lifetimes I had worked with my guides. Did the guides have different hierarchies? How many types of guides were there? Then it occurred to me to ask, "What was the difference between angels and a guides?" How did they interact and support me in different ways?

Most of the books I read about were on angels or archangels. It occurred to me that the title "angel" was a broadly used definition used to represent divine entities that were assisting us. But I was finding through my channeling practice that there were many different types of angels. And that angels and guides had different purposes.

I also learned that angels and guides had different levels of strength, and that teams turned over when we moved up in the Ascension process. As I was advancing in my practice, I was alerted when new guides came on to my team. At a certain point in my development, I was told I would only be working with guides. Then, as time marched on and my spiritual practice evolved, I was introduced to the Ascended Masters. In my current evolution, I work with the Guardians and Lords of Karma. But that's another story, for a different book.

What I discovered was that angels and guides have different roles. Angels perform tasks and assist a person in life. Depending on the evolution of the person, some people are surrounded by their angels. Especially if they constantly ask for help and invite them into their auric field. Angels give positive messages. They send loving and kind thoughts throughout the day. They remind you to eat healthily, or will say, "Don't eat that, you know it's not good for you." Angels are sweet and provide comfort.

Angels encourage spiritual practice. They remind you to go to yoga or tunein online for a meditation. I learned how angels work to protect my auric field and clear my chakra system of energy debris that I picked up during the day. I also found out that angels communicate with guides. If they feel I need something urgently or want a change in direction, they alert the guides to pay attention and get involved.

Spirit guides are different. They are more serious in nature. They don't do tasks like the angels. They are more like professors, counselors and guides. They occasionally hold council meetings to discuss one's progress. I learned they listen to prayer requests. They decide about job placements and appropriate friends and romantic relationships. They decide which workshops one should attend and what spiritual teachers will benefit you.

They were watching my life unfold and watching over me to make sure I stayed on course with my life purpose. I learned they had specialties. One day I was at a bookstore and a book nearly fell off the shelf as I was browsing. The book was on hypnosis. When I got home, I asked, "Who dropped this book?". It was the guide that was teaching me meditation. She felt I was ready to expand my practice and learn about hypnosis.

I also learned that guides do not become involved with people who are not yet ready to receive the benefit of spiritual growth. People who are disinterested in spirituality only have one guide, their guardian angel. If a person starts to pray or finds a spiritual path, then the guides take interest and will get involved. But if a person is disinterested, they take a back seat and wait until someone starts to pray about how they can heal themselves or heal other people.

In the material below, I define the different types of angels and guides. Using the pendulum communication tool, I found detailed information about my angels and guides.

Much of the information that I received I wrote about in the book **10 Cosmic Dimensions, A Spiritual Guidebook to Ascension**. I have enjoyed asking countless questions about the hierarchies of angels and guides, past lives, karma and other items I have found interesting over the years.

Younger Souls and Advanced Souls

For many years I have been reading clients to find out how many angels and guides are in their auric field or working with them directly. What I have found is that there are big differences in the angelic teams between younger souls and advanced souls.

Younger souls are on the wheel of karma. They are learning lessons about heart issues and being a good person. They are either not interested in spirituality or they follow traditional religious teachings. They understand about Divine Source in simple ways. Younger souls have incarnated just on Earth, over the last 4000 years or more. Their soulful intention is to graduate to ascension in the Light Realms.

Most advanced souls are not on the wheel of karma. Most advanced souls have been incarnating on several higher frequency planets in addition to Earth. There is one category of advanced souls that is still on the wheel of karma: advanced angels. Other representatives from the astral realms have incarnated and have no karma or baggage to deal with. These advanced souls are volunteers. In New Age literature they have been titled indigos, rainbow, crystalline, starseeds and several other titles defining different generations and traits. They come in clear and with psychic skills. In this work, all groupings are called lightworkers.

The volunteers are not here because of their karma. They are here because they heard the call. The Ascended Masters asked those in the Light Realms, "Who among you will volunteer to go to Earth at this time of transition and assist in any way you can to bring love and light to the dark world?" Many heard the call and decided to incarnate on Earth, knowing how dangerous and uncomfortable the mission would be. Volunteers normally feel out of place in this world and wonder, "How did a loving soul like me, end up on a dangerous and dark planet like this?"

What I found was that younger souls had one guide. What the Christian Bible calls the guardian angel. The number of angels on the team varied from 0 to 5 to 19. The number of angels depended on the soul's interest in growing in the light and their spiritual practice. It also depended on if they were calling on their angels and if the person needed angelic support. If the soul had no interest in spiritual growth or was overwhelmed with dark energy, there would be no angels in the field and plenty of negative energy.

For the advanced souls, the angel readings were totally different. Advanced souls that incarnated for the mission will have 40, 50 or even 100 guides watching over them on their team depending on the scope of their work. Angels have a less significant role on the team, with the exception of clearing the chakras and protecting against negative energy.

Advanced souls with large guide teams normally have 1 to 4 guides interacting with them daily. In addition angels, Archangels or guardians are assigned for clearing the energy body and protecting against negativity. If you are seeing angel number signs or are aware of other undeniable synchronicities, your guides are in your auric field or chakra system and are trying to get your attention. Guides are very active with advanced souls, especially when they become aware of who they are and their potential to be healers or helpers in the world.

Guides understand advanced souls will wake up with amnesia and not remember who they are or why they incarnated on Earth. The guides assist in accelerated growth and moving lightworkers along in the Ascension process. Guides want their candidates to awaken and get to work as soon as possible. Guides grant psychic skills according to the candidate's awareness and life purpose. Guides have specialties in astrology, numerology, pranic healing, crystals, meditation, arts and divination work. Some guides are more practical to the 3rd dimensional world. They assist with business projects, manifesting engineering projects, starting non-profits intended to help the community.

The guides start to work with candidates they sent down to Earth to do a mission. The younger souls don't really need a lot of spirit guides because they are not interested in learning spiritual information or advancing in healing work. The advanced souls are different; they are attuned to the vibrations of higher frequencies and are interested in subjects that are not of this world.

I have noticed that younger souls, especially ones with good karma, can ask to be healers and the guides will consider them for the work and promote them.

This is a very difficult time period on Earth. Everyone who is willing to be helpful or of service will be put to work to do something positive in the world. With a sincere prayer, the guidance team will increase in number and an appropriate life purpose will be granted.

How Many Angels are in my Field?

If you have a regular spiritual practice and are working with your angels, then your angelic team is surrounding you because you have asked for assistance and protection. If you are new to spiritual path and want to start working with your angels, remember you have to ask for assistance and call them into your field.

Occasionally, I will do an angel reading and find out that a person only has one or two or no angels in their auric field assisting them. I know from doing many readings that this number is too small, they should have more angels in their auric field. The next question I will ask is, "How many angels are supposed to be in the field?" If they are supposed to have 20 angels in their field, but only three are present, I will ask that the angels assigned them to come back into their field.

I learned early on in my practice that angels don't sit on the bench. Everyone is assigned a number of angels to assist them, but if we are not utilizing them or not calling on them they will go to where they are needed. Imagine that you are assigned twenty angels, but you are not yet awake or working with them. They will not hang around. They will go where they are needed until you are ready to utilize them.

Angels, at this time on Earth, are in shorter supply due to the increase in weather changes and more violence on the Earth. We have to ask them to stay with us through our intentions and prayers.

Imagine there is a natural disaster. A church group might pray for a state or country in need. Literally, angels assigned to you that are not being useful, or are considered to be sitting on the bench, will hear the call of the prayer and be reassigned to leave you to go where they can be helpful. Another scenario is that you are feeling very healthy and are full of gratitude. Your chakras are clear, everything is positive and working out for you. The guidance team may feel you can spare the angels, and will send them to be helpful where they are needed.

Angels are literary deployed to Earth, in much the same way that the military deploys to other countries. The angels that service the Earth have homes in the Light Realms. They are also volunteers to the Earth, and take shifts serving the humans here. That being said, there is a finite number of angels. Angels are moved around by the commanding Archangels to places on Earth where they are needed. Especially at this time period on Earth, angels, if you can imagine, are working overtime.

Through my channelings I have learned that angels might be assigned to three or four humans. That way if one person is underutilizing the angels on their team, those angels will go to another person that is calling them into their field.

Remember that the angels can only assist us if we invite them in. If you are having a hard time, but haven't requested the support of your angelic team, say a prayer and invite them back into your field.

On Earth, negative energy doesn't need our permission to invade our energy field. Angels and the Ascended Masters, on the other hand are different. They want us to attune to them and invite them in. They want us to choose love and light according to our own free will.

Call In More Protection and Clearing Angels

The other reason why there may not be enough angels in your field is because you are surrounded by toxic negative energy in your home or work place. Many people live with unhealthy family members. If you live with someone with a drug or alcohol problem or someone who has a mental illness, it is likely that protection angels are working hard to protect you. You may have fewer angels because they are constantly guarding against negative energy entering your field.

Your protection angels will guard your field from negative energy, but if you are in a dark or toxic environment the protection team might be outnumbered or overwhelmed. Try to imagine what this looks like on the 5th dimensional astral plane. Your field is bright and angels are standing at the ready to protect you. If a negative energy comes in, a protection angel will engage it. Usually both energies will be neutralized.

If you are in the habit of calling in an Archangel or an Ascended Master for protection that is an appropriate practice. If you need an Archangel they will come to your side. This teaching clarifies that in addition to the Archangels, you have a personal team. If you are a lightworker or energy healer, your team is working with you every day, whether you call in an Archangel or not. My experience with the Archangels is that they are commanders. They lead troops of protection angels. For example, if you call in Archangel Michael, your protection team stands at the ready. Your personal angelic team knows you need assistance. If the stronger energy of Archangel Michael is needed, a commanding angel will come to your aid.

Many people work in negative energy work environments. For example, if you work in a hospital, the criminal justice system or military, you are working in trauma environments that are swarming with negative energies. You may not realize it, but you may experience negative psychic attacks to your auric field and chakra system. Negative energy swarms around trauma environments and other dark environments like nightclubs and bars.

Lightworkers have a bigger and brighter auric field than someone who is not working with their angels. If a lightworker walks into a bar, every negative energy in the room will notice the person's auric field is brighter than the rest. A negative energy might muse, "What on Earth is an angelic human doing in a dark environment like this?"

If the lightworker drinks too much alcohol, their auric field opens and negative energy is likely to attack. Literally, a negative energy will create a chakra wound and dark energy will enter the energy body through the wound. If the wound stays open, it's like a hole that can let other negative energies into your field. Chakra wounds are discussed in the book **100 Chakra System**. I have discovered that if the environment is dark enough, it doesn't matter if you are sober or not, negative energy will attack.

As long as you have a strong energy clearing and meditation practice, you will invite pranic flow into your field. This will align your chakra system, repair your auric field and restore your angelic team. Astral beings do not die as we do. Since they live infinite lives, if they go to battle protecting us and are injured, they move into a light chamber to restore. Angels don't die, they "restore". Angels come back to life, but this can take days or weeks in our time, depending on the type of angels.

If you know you work in a toxic negative energy environment or live with negative people you can ask, "How many protection angels do I have in my field?" "Do I need more protection angels?" If the answer is yes, ask, "How many protection angels will you send to me?" "Do I need to call in stronger angels?" "Do I need to leave this situation?"

Clearing angels clear the chakra system of negative energies. Make sure you have enough angels for whatever circumstances you are dealing with. If you are an energy healer and you are clearing people's chakra systems with pranic flow, then your guides will naturally put more angels into your field.

If you feel uncomfortable energy in your chakra system, make sure to ask, "How many clearing angels do I have in my field?" "Do I need more clearing angels to do my healing work, or deal with negative energy in my work place or at home?"

Another reason to ask for more clearing angels is that your chakra system is clearing itself out. Once you start to practice energy work, or become conscious that you want to clear your 100 chakras towards ascension, your clearing angels, or guides will start to clear your higher chakras. Your energy body will start to clear subconscious material or past life traumas. Negative energies harbor in these chakra clusters. Negative energies can move within the chakra line. They might be hiding up in the chakra clusters and then move down into the seven chakras, where they can be felt in your present moment.

If a negative energy is up in the chakra system, you don't experience that energy directly. You might experience it through nightmares or subconscious fears.

But if the negative energy moves downward into your seven chakras, then it becomes a part of your present reality.

Now you are experiencing that energy as a depression or a feeling of aggression in your daily life. Your clearing angels will help you with this. If you are asking for help and meditating with the intention of clearing your chakra system, clearing angels will neutralize negative energies.

Chapter 6.   Learn the Names of Your Angels

Naming Angels and Guides

It is helpful and beneficial to know and form relationships with your angelic team. Remember, when you call on your angels or guides by name, they always come to your side. Of course, you don't need to know the names of your angels to have them come to you. You can always just pray or ask for help, and the appropriate support will come. Knowing their names simply helps strengthen and solidify the relationship, making their presence more tangible in our physical reality.

When I started to channel in my angel names, I got unusual names. I learned that not all names come to people in English. The first guide name I channeled in was Sortiforus. I politely asked, "Can I give you a nickname?" He answered "Yes", and became known to me as Sorf.

If you feel you channeled in a strange name, you can ask if you can give the angel or guide a nickname. A few times, I have guides tell me they prefer their formal name. One time I channeled in the name Sosa Martin. I asked him, "Can I call you Sosa or Martin?" He said, "No". Out of respect for his wishes I called him by his full name. He was known to me as Sosa Martin.

Many times the guides will use English names or names that are familiar to your culture in order to relate to you. The guides will know intuitively what kind of names should be presented to you. I have known advanced souls who have received interesting and unique names. Likewise those less developed on the spiritual path will get simple name like Sara and Daniel. You will receive exactly what you need at your level of spiritual evolution.

I also understood that I was channeling in the names phonetically as it might sound in English. For fun, I include below one of my early lists of angel names that I channeled in years ago. As it turns out, I am no longer working with these angels, as my spiritual attunement has evolved. But it gives you an example. And remember, if the names make no sense at all, go back and use the validation questions. In my example list, "F" is for female and "M" is for male. It is also possible to get an angel or guide that identifies as "A" for androgyny, meaning they do not identify with a gender.

Names of my Angels

Estara (F) Healing Angel
Past Life, Crystals, Clearing Negative Energies from people

Ariel (F) Healing Angel
Healing Clients, Clearing Entities from People, Healing Tools

Daniel (M) Protection Angel
Leader of the Protection Team

Leguemasl (M) Healing Angel
Writing, Communication, Angel Readings

Gadilino (F) Protection Angel
Vocation, Creation, 2-D Art, Creator, Developing my Career

Kunvc (F) Healing Angel
Vocation, Counseling

Mickrvvuv (F)
Creative Arts, Helps with Signing

Manorkyy (A) Service Angel
Service to the World, Helping create the Audience

Ziquel (M) Divination Arts
Time Lines and Potential Outcomes, synchronicity, Card Reading, Palm Reading, Numerology, Scribing, Crystal Gazing, channeling, tea leaves

Rikbiel (M)
Spiritual Practice, Knowledge of God, Sacred Literature

Zenda (A)
Astral Angel of Health and Healing, Abundance and Manifesting

3 Pendulum Charts for Meeting Your Angelic Team

In this section of the book, three charts are presented to assist you in finding out more about your angelic team. The first chart is the Alphabet Chart, the second chart is the Number Chart and the third chart is titled Types of Angels and Guides. Working with charts is the easiest form of pendulum work. Traditional pendulum charts have the words YES, NO, MAYBE or REPHRASE on them. People can usually get the pendulum to swing to a Yes or a No. For this work we want to program the pendulum for Yes and No responses.

Programming the pendulum means you tell your angels what the movement of the pendulum means to you so that you can communicate it clearly. Ask the pendulum to make a clockwise circle at the center of the alphabet chart, tell your guidance team, this means "Yes". Then ask the pendulum to make a horizontal line. Tell your angels this means "No".

Next we are going to use the Alphabet Chart and the Number Chart together to learn the names of your angels and guides. To avoid interference or getting bad answers first clear your auric field and your chakra system. Remember, just because you can get the pendulum to move, doesn't necessarily mean you are channeling your guides.

Go to your sacred space. A sacred space is somewhere in your home where you sit to meditate. It should be clear of debris and feel comfortable to you. There should be no one else in the room with you when you attempt to channel.

A sacred space contains an altar that you sit in front of to meditate. An altar is a table that contains your Divine symbols and tools. An altar helps to define a peaceful and angelic space in your home. It is a place for spiritual practice and a place for your spiritual tools.

On the altar, place symbols that remind you of the Divine and your spiritual practice. Ideas for an altar include candles and personal symbols that remind you of the Divine. Many people place images or sculptures of the Ascended Masters and other Divine representatives on their altars. Prayer requests can be written on a paper or in a journal and placed on the altar. Many people place their pendulum, oracle cards or other divination tools on their altar or scared space.

A white crystal can help to hold angelic energy and create a field that keeps interference energy out of the room. I recommend a large selenite tower at least 4 inches tall or larger. This helps create an angelic energy field. A large quartz crystal will also create an angelic energetic field. Imagine that when you sit at the altar, the auric field of the large white crystal starts to expand and the energy field of white light is all around you.

Sit in your sacred space and hold the intention to clear your auric field and clear your chakra system so that you are clear enough to channel. It is recommended that you clear your energy field through meditation for 20 minutes before you attempt to channel. A chakra clearing meditation is ideal for this. There are chakra meditations on my YouTube channel, search 'Raven Shamballa Chakra Clearing Meditation'. This practice will elevate your consciousness and shake off the energy of your day. Meditation will move you into an ascended relaxed state, which is ideal for contacting your angels.

Now you are ready to attempt spirit communication with your angelic team. Intend to connect with your angels and guides. Start by asking the validation questions. Hold the pendulum over the Number Chart. Ask, "Am I clear enough to channel?" If you get a "Yes" the pendulum makes a clockwise circle. You are clear to move forward. If you get a "No" a horizontal line, left to right, that means there is a form of interference. If you get a "No" ask, "Should I meditate longer?" If you get a "Yes", sit for another 15 minutes and ask again.

Start with the number chart. Ask the following question. "How many angels would like to give their name?" Allow the pendulum to swing to the appropriate number. You may get the response, "1" or "3" or a different number. For most people that answer will be "1". Next ask the question, "How many letters are in your name?" Write down or remember your answer. Next ask, "How many syllables are in your name? Write down or remember your answer.

Next move to the alphabet chart. Now we know what we are looking for. As an example imagine that you got the answer five letters and one syllable. Find the first letter. Hold the pendulum and allow the instrument to move to the correct letter. Imagine you got "S". Channel in the rest of the names. You receive the name Sarah.

When you first start this work, you may need to go slowly and spell out all the letters. As you advance try to practice clairaudience. Clairaudience is the psychic ability to hear the angel name or messages from your angels without using the tool of the pendulum. In this example, if the first letter that you received is "S" listen and see if you hear the rest of the name before you channel in all the letters. As I developed in the work, the names would pop into my head after I got the first letter. In this way the pendulum is a helpful tool for developing clairaudience.

If you have a "how" or "why" question, you can try to rephrase it into a "yes/no" question, or another solution is to meditate deeply and ask for the answer to the question. The purpose of this work is to develop intuitive guidance and hear your answer. The pendulum has limitations. Ultimately you want to hear and understand what you are asking about. Remember to listen, messages will come to you. At first these messages are like whispers, but over time they are more audible and you know it's your angels speaking to you.

Types of Angels and Guides

The next chart is called Types of Angels and Guides. I created this chart over time to understand how my personal angelic team was assisting me. The information below outlines what I discovered. Angels and guides have specialties. As we learn new skills, different angelic energies come forward to assist us.

Next go to the Angel Type chart. Ask the question, "Are you an Angel or a Spirit Guide?" The pendulum will swing left or right to the correct merkabah cube. If it swings to the left, it's an angel and if it swings to the right, it's a guide. Next ask the questions, "What type of angel are you?" or ask, "How do you assist me?" Allow the pendulum to swing to the merkabah cube behind the words describing the types of angels. Now you know your angel's name and also how this angelic being assists you.

If you get a strange name and you want to know the gender of the angel, ask if the angelic being is masculine, feminine or androgynous in nature. Program the merkabah cube to the left to mean female, program the merkabah cube to the right to mean male and program the center angel wings to mean androgyny or not expressing a masculine or feminine quality.

Next find out how the angel is specialized to assist you. There are two arches with the descriptive words. Ask the pendulum to move to the merkabah cube behind the correct word. This will help you distinguish which arc the pendulum is moving towards. As your ability to move the pendulum improves, you intuitively know which arch the pendulum is swinging to. If you are still unsure if you have the correct descriptive word, hold the pendulum over the word. You can validate your answers with a Yes/No swing. If you get a "Yes" clockwise swing over the word you will validate your answer is correct.

The key for the types of angels and guides are outlined on pages 40-41. After you use the pendulum chart to find out what types of angels are working with you, refer to the Angel Type Pendulum Key to get more information. This chart uses a double arch. Program the pendulum tip to go to the star image behind the word on the double arches. I use the word 'angels' in the title, but these descriptions include spirit guides as well. Spirit guides have specialties and are more like professors in their subject areas.

Additional Purposes for Using the Number and Alphabet Charts

The alphabet and number charts can be used for a variety of purposes and for asking questions. You can use your imagination to start having conversations with your angelic team. Other questions you might ask are, "What is the total number of guides on my team?" "How many guides are working with me today?" "How long have you been working with me?" Between each question, pause and listen. Remember the goal is clairaudience and the pendulum is just a tool to assist you in the process. If you listen between questions, you will be surprised at the information that you might receive.

Also some people are developing the skill of clairaudience and might be better at seeing with their inner vision or imagination. In this case, between each question and answer close your eyes, turn your gaze up and focus at the point between the eyebrows. A vision may come to you. In guided meditation or hypnosis sessions that I lead, people often see or imagine their angels. Other people who are developed in clairsentience just know things. They will know that there are three angels to the left and two to the right. They can feel or sense them.

On one of the alphabet charts, there are angel wing symbols in each of the four corners. You can also program the four angel symbols. Programming means that you assign meaning to the symbol. For example, imagine you know that you are working with three angels named Sarah, Jeremy and Paul. Assign the angel wing on the upper left corner to mean Sarah, assign the upper right corner to Jeremy, and assign the lower right corner to be Paul.

Later in your practice you can ask questions like, "Who is working with me today?" or "Who gave me the angel sign this afternoon?" Watch which corner the pendulum swings to. You can make personal markings on the chart to mean different things in order to get more information. You are encouraged to make photocopies of the charts, and should feel free to write on them. Use your imagination to write on the charts to get more information about your angels or other topics that are interesting to you.

You can use the number chart to receive all kinds of information pertaining to numbers. The trick here is to understand how many digits are in the number. Is the number in the tenths place, the hundredths place, or the thousandths place? The purpose of the bottom arc is to help you find that answer to how many digits you are looking for in your answer.

You can ask, "How many digits are in my answer?" and allow the pendulum to swing to the 1, 10, 100, 1000 or 10,000. You can also hold the pendulum over the digits and ask that the correct number make a clockwise circle meaning "Yes". For example, if 10 was the correct answer, the pendulum would make a circle over that number. The other number would show a line or "No" answer. You can also ask percentage questions using the number chart. Just intend that the top row means % and allow the pendulum to swing to the correct answer. If it goes to the number 7, that would mean 70%.

You can use the alphabet chart to ask questions about mediumship. This book doesn't cover the topic of mediumship, but I will mention one thing here. Many advanced souls will hold fragments of lost souls. A lost soul is an earth-bound spirit. I discuss this topic in the 100 Chakra Book. I bring it up here because you may ask the question, "Is this an Angel or a Guide?" and instead of the pendulum swinging to the correct answer, it may swing counter clockwise or to an area that you didn't intend. In this case, you could very well be channeling a lost soul rather than an entity from your angelic team.

If this is the case, don't panic. There is nothing to fear. You might go back to validation questions, "Is this a negative energy?" or "Is this a lost soul?" If you ask that question and get a "Yes", invite the lost soul to cross over to the Light Realms. Ask the appropriate angel on your team to assist the lost soul in going over to the other side. As a beginner there is not much more you need to do than sit and meditate for 20 minutes. At the end of the meditation ask the validation questions again.

A free color download of the Types of Angels and Guides chart is also available on the website. If you would like a designed color chart of the Alphabet or Numbers you can order them separately at **www.ravenlightbody.com**.

More Questions to Ask When Learning the Names of Your Angels

Below is an outline of questions you can ask your angelic team through using the Alphabet Chart and the Number Chart. Before you begin, remember to first ask the validation questions.

First meditate for 10 to 15 minutes then ask the pendulum the following questions:
- Am I clear enough to channel?
- Should I meditate longer?

If you get a Yes, sit for another 15 minutes and ask again.
- Is this a negative energy?
- Am I a female?
- Should I jump off a bridge?

Have fun discovering information about your angelic team.
- How many angels are on my team?
- How many letters are in your name?
- Are you male, female or androgynous?
- Would you mind if I give you a nickname?
- What is a word that describes how you help me?
- How many letters are in the word?
- How long have you been working with me?
- Have I ever channeled you before?
- Are you an angel or a spirit guide or something else?

If something else, ask validation questions or ask if it's an Archangel or Ascended Master. You can also ask if they are a lost soul, or earth-bound spirit.
- How many guides are on my team?
- How many digits are there in the total number?
- How many angels or guides worked with me today?
- How many angels are supposed to be in my auric field?
- What is the total number of protection angels in my field?
- How many protection angels do I have in my field today?
- How many clearing angels do I have in my field?
- Do I have enough clearing angels to do my healing work?
- Do I have enough clearing angels to deal with negative energy in my work place or at home?

Developing Clairaudience
- Use the pendulum to get the first letter of the name.
- Next tune inward and listen; try to anticipate the name of the angel.
- If you get the letter "S", see what name comes to you.
- To validate ask a Yes/No question. Is this your name?
- Practice listening before the pendulum completes its swing.

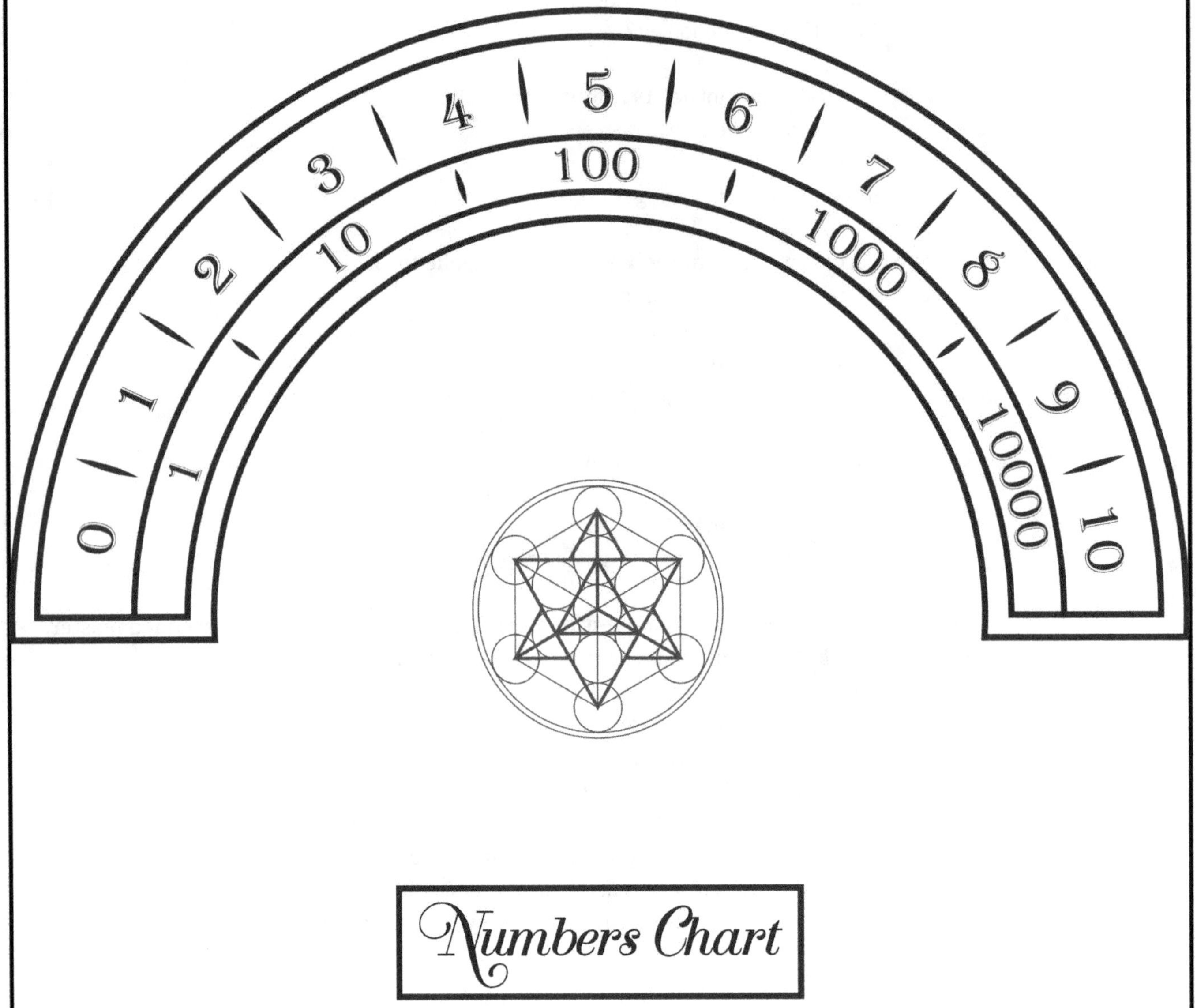

0 | 1 | 2 | 3 | 4 | 5 | 6 | 7 | 8 | 9 | 10
10 | 100 | 1000 | 10000

Numbers Chart

www.ravenlightbody.com

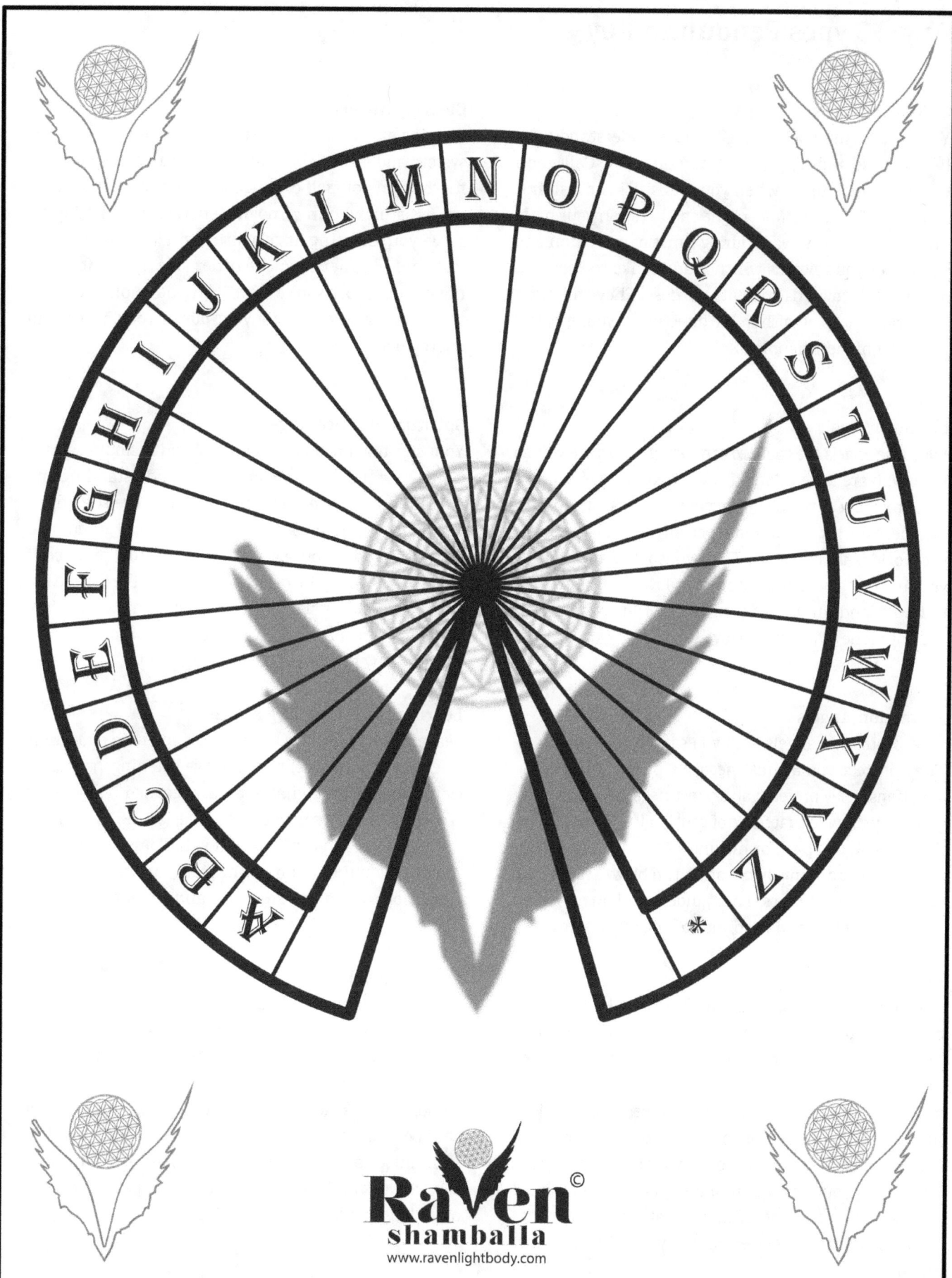

Angel Types Pendulum Key

Guidance Angels
Your guardian angel or spirit guides understand your life purpose and help you to stay on track. Call upon your guidance team when you feel stuck, or lost and confused. They will shine a light and brighten your path. The guides come forward during times of indecision and will direct you towards which road to take to keep you on the path towards your life purpose. They will often encourage a leap of faith in the direction of your greatest good and highest happiness.

Comfort Angels
Your love angels are there to comfort and nurture you, so know you are never alone. They support and encourage you, providing a friendly feeling in times of sadness. They are there during transition especially when it feels as if the world is falling apart. They will soothe and console you so you feel warm all over. Your love angels help you to find friends and open your heart. You are held, you are not alone, and you are loved.

Protection Angels
Your protection angels keep you safe from harm's way. They protect you against negative people, places, and situations. They protect you against negative astral energies. They provide that voice of caution if you are moving down the wrong path or making wrong decisions. They protect you from injury or soften the blow. They shield you from the darkness. They guide your journey when you are traveling and keep you safe during dreamtime.

Healing Angels
Your healing angels work specifically on healing your own personal issues. They guide you towards spiritual teachers, counselors and healers. They are with you when you are on the mend from injury. They assist you to grow, reflect and consider your choices and decisions in life situations. Healing angels care deeply about your state of being, your physical body, your emotional health and getting you back into balance after a difficult period. They are the voice that tells you to eat this and not that, relax - calm down. They encourage you to be in balance on all levels of your being.

Clearing Angels
Clearing angels remove energy debris from your chakra system and auric field. If you practice an energy healing method on yourself or on clients, your clearing angels are assisting you in removing energies that no longer serve you. Clearing angels also assist in crossing over lost soul fragments to the other side. If you feel you have seen a lost soul or felt it in your home, call on the clearing angels to move it out of your home and energy body.

Spiritual Practice Angels
Your spiritual practice angels assist you in finding a path or practice that will accelerate your understanding and perception of the enlightenment. They are the angels that guide you to books, lead you to spiritual groups and programs and encourage your daily spiritual practice. If you are guided in the direction of meditation, these are the angels that assist in quieting your mind. They are there to help you grow and understand who you really are and how to live in the light every day.

Learning and Teaching Angels
Learning and teaching angels assist you with education. They assist the student with active listening, participation and applying what you have learned. They assist the teacher in strong communication skills, sharing their wisdom and continued growth. These angels assist in educational environments, from formal schools, to workshops, to online programs and retreat centers.

Service Angels
Service angels guide you in the direction of helping other people. They are the voice inside that asks, "How can I help?" They create synchronicity to help you find opportunities that will best help you in your service to the world. Service angels encourage service missions, whether that be volunteering at the local soup kitchen, or adding your unique skill set to help others. They assist with your service work and guide you toward your passion to lend a helping hand.

Angel Types Pendulum Key

Divination Angels
Divination angels guide you to spiritual tools and methods of practice in the divination arts. They assist you in understanding what tools might be best for you. They assist you in flipping divination cards, learning astrology, numerology, crystals, and other spiritual tools you find interesting. They add an element of magic in your life and help you relate to others through the discovery of hidden knowledge. Divination angels keep you connected to the spirit world through interaction and play.

Angels in the Healing Arts
Angels that work in the healing arts guide your path as a healer. They encourage your healing work and want you to bring light to the world. They guide you towards your best method of healing others, like bodywork, counseling, nutrition, chiropractic, acupuncture or medicine to name a few. They inspire you towards healthy living and finding a practice that will help you heal others. They come in to assist you while you are healing those around you.

Angels in the Elemental Arts
Angels that work in the elemental arts assist you with getting back to the Earth. They love nature and inspire you to find your beach, mountain top or sunset. They encourage you to garden, make teas and other natural remedies. These are the angels that urge one to plant a tree, nurture a flower bed, or plant an herb garden. They care deeply for the Earth, and want us to feel the soil beneath our feet, breathe fresh air and be inspired by nature.

Creative Angels
Creative arts angels inspire your creativity. They know your talents and gifts and want you to make or do something marvelous and artistic. They encourage you in the direction of painting, singing, dancing, and the theatrical arts. They want you to flow with divine creative energy and be the co-creator that manifests beautiful and colorful works of art. They encourage you in the direction of your creative passion and know that you feel inspired when you engage in your artistic endeavors.

Angels supporting Psychic Gifts
Psychic gift angels help to awaken your psychic abilities. They project images to you during guided visualizations. They strengthen your intuition and help you to trust your knowingness of what's right intuitively. They come in to assist you with clairvoyance, clairaudience, precognition and dream interpretation to name a few. They help us with telepathy and knowing mystical knowledge beyond our five senses and conscious mind.

Vocation Angels
Vocation angels help you with your monetary work. They understand that we need money as an exchange for abundance in our current creation. They help us find vocations that are best suited to us. They assist us in learning new skills, networking, gaining employment or starting a business. They are practical and guide our paths in the direction of our best professional work. They are very active during times of career transitions and assist in moving us forward in our work.

Technology Angels
Technology angels help us with computers, cell phones, monitors, new software applications and other technological advancements. They assist us in figuring out new technology. They tell us to be brave when approaching a new technology and help us not get too frustrated when we don't understand what to do or feel uncomfortable with the new application. They understand how fast our world has been advancing and they are here to help us stay on track with technological advancement.

Business Angels
Business angels understand all aspects of business and help us with accounting, marketing, networking, finding clients, working with team members and manifesting projects. If you are an employee, they assist with team communication, project management and moving in the direction of a successful outcome. If you are a business owner or want to start a business, they assist with helping you find the right resources, making bold decisions, taking risks and building your own creation.

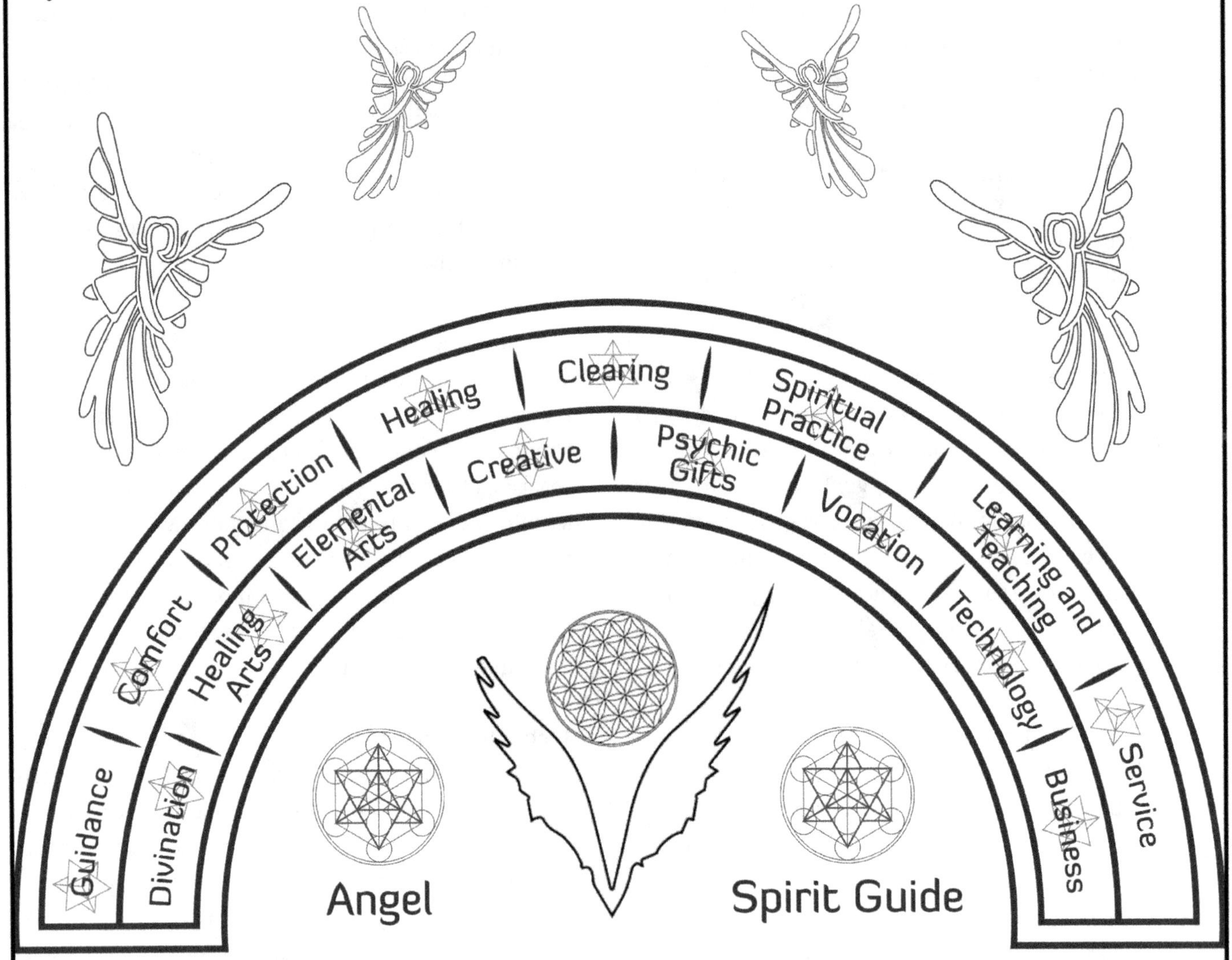

Angel Types

Guidance | Divination | Healing Arts | Comfort | Protection | Elemental Arts | Healing | Creative | Clearing | Psychic Gifts | Spiritual Practice | Vocation | Learning and Teaching | Technology | Business | Service

Angel | Spirit Guide

www.ravenlightbody.com

Chapter 7.   Pendulum on the Hand

How the Pendulum Language Developed

After graduate school, I started working with private clients. After a client would leave the session, I would start to ask the guides questions about the energy healing. I would want to know, "What was happening during the chakra clearing? How many angels or guides were working with me? How much did the client improve in terms of healing? Did I use the correct affirmations, are there other affirmations I should use?" I would wait to hear a message.

I had also started the practice of chakra balancing. I wanted to know, "What chakras were cleared? Why did it take more time to clear certain chakras and not others? How many treatments did my angelic team feel the client needed to clear their issue?" The topic of chakra balancing is covered in the next book in this series called, **Chakra Balancing with the Pendulum**. This is a topic unto itself. The questions were endless for me. I kept asking questions and the answers kept coming. I wrote down the answers keeping notes and journals. This is how I produced the book the **100 Chakra System**, which is the foundational book for this style of energy healing, called Negative Energy Release Work.

At a certain point, I got tired of working with charts and needed to go faster. Charts were good for gathering information and getting more details quickly, but it wasn't very fast when I wanted quick information. I started to pendulum on my hand. My five fingers and other markers on the hand could replace the charts. As my channeling and question-and-answer sessions got more sophisticated, so did the language with my guides.

At this point in my career, I considered myself highly intuitive, but not completely psychic. I could receive messages, but still relied heavily on the pendulum which was easy and fast for me to get information. This was twelve years before my first psychic opening, when I became completely clairaudient. Now I have no need for the pendulum except to demonstrate it to those who want to learn how to use it. But at this time in my development I would pick up the pendulum several times in the day to clear myself and the office, and then to ask questions about the healing work.

In this chapter, I share how I used my left hand, my non-dominant hand, as a surface to get information, instead of using a chart. The short-grip hold of the pendulum is better when swinging the instrument on your hand. A short-grip hold means the dominant hand, the right hand, pinches the string of the pendulum about 1 or 2 inches above the weighted pendulum object. This allows the pendulum to move fast and make accurate movements. This is in contrast to the long-grip hold in which you hold the pendulum at the top and allow it to dangle. The pendulum will make longer slower movements. This hold can be easier for beginners to get the pendulum to swing.

I also preferred a lighter crystal pendulum for this method of communication, rather than a heavy metal pendulum. A metal heavy pendulum is better for being accurate on the chart surface. The metal pendulum is easier to move for beginners because it is heavier and easy to feel. The lighter pendulum, usually made from crystal, is better for quick, short distance movements on the palm of the hand. Also, I used the lighter crystal pendulums for chakra balancing because it was very easy to twirl and read the chakras and the outer auric field. Metal pendulums are not good for twirling quickly or reading chakras.

At the end of this section, I give the pendulum commands that I use on the surface of the palm of my left hand. These commands create the language for angelic communication. As you advance in spirit communication the movement of the pendulum becomes more fluid like a dialog. The language of pendulum on the hand assumes you can get the pendulum to move easily and have learned how to use the pendulum with charts.

Programming the Pendulum on the Hand

As you move through the hand illustrations, you can program the pendulum movements. You and your angelic team become clear on what you intend the movements to mean. This is called programming the pendulum. This will give you and your angelic team the common language for communication.

Since the majority of people are right-handed, I consider the right hand to be the dominant hand, holding the pendulum, and the left hand to be the non-dominant hand, creating the surface for the pendulum to move on. If you are left-handed, you may need to make adjustments. We'll use the "Show Me" command, to practice moving the pendulum with your guidance team.

The "Show Me" command is a way to clearly communicate with your angelic team. You are speaking to your guidance team and asking them to "Show you" the communications you intend. Hold the pendulum with your dominant hand using the short grip. Place your non-dominant hand underneath to produce a surface. Say out loud, "Show me Yes". The pendulum will make a clockwise circle. Both you and the guidance team practice making the pendulum move. As we move through the diagrams, use the "Show Me" command after each section to program the pendulum. Make sure to include asking questions you already know the answer to, in order to see if the intended swing is the same.

For beginners, it is easier to program the left-hand surface first using your pointer finger. Take the pointer finger of your right hand and trace the meaning of the swing on the left hand. Do this a few times, before you try to make the pendulum move. Often the movement is very small, but the student can feel the pendulum is moving as they intend it to. Remember if the movement is small, using a metal pendulum is recommended. The heavy weight is easier to feel and move. If you are skilled already at using a pendulum, you can program the commands using your pendulum.

After you trace the movements say the commands. Next, pick up the pendulum and use the "Show Me" command. Say out loud "Show me Yes", "Show me No", "Show me Not Yet", "Show me Not Really", "Show me Not Able to Tell You Yet." You are asking your spirit guide team to make the pendulum move, you are also intending the meanings of each movement. In this way you are learning the language and are practicing moving the pendulum.

If you are left-handed, the "Show Me" commands may produce a different outcome than what is shown on the diagrams. When I have tried to use my left hand as the dominant hand holding the pendulum, I notice that the swings are backwards than what I intended. Everyone is different! Go with what the guides show you. The information here is a guideline to help you get started. Take the information and evolve it to make it your own.

Orientation, Yes, No, Not Really, Not Yet

Let's start to program the pendulum. Take a look at the hand charts at the end of this chapter. The first diagram is called, "Orientation". This diagram gives the orientation of the left-hand surface. There are nine points on the hand. Take your right finger and touch each of the nine points. You know the numbers for the five fingers. Point six is on the inside middle of the palm, seven is at the right corner of the palm, eight is the center of the wrist and nine is the center of the hand.

These positions will be used as we move through the hand diagrams. This way we can be very accurate with the pendulum swing. Make your left hand as flat as possible to make an accurate surface. You may want to take a marker and write on the surface of the hand to assist you in remembering the numbered positions. This is a fast way to learn the pendulum language on the hand. Practice the orientation positions. Say out loud, "Show me finger 1", then "Show me finger 2". Move through the 9 positions and make the pendulum move to all the positions on the hand.

Next trace the basic movement of "Yes" and "No", diagrams 2 and 3. A clockwise circle means "Yes" and a vertical line from the middle finger (**finger 3**) to the center of the wrist (**position 8**) means "No".

The next pendulum command is "Not Really" or "Not Yet". The pendulum movement is shown in diagram 4.

This command is a diagonal line from the pointer finger (**finger 2**) to the right corner of the palm (**position 8**). I call the "Not Really" diagonal line a "double negative" answer because it follows a "No" swing. The guides will answer, "No" a vertical line, and then "Not Really" a diagonal line. Or they will answer, "No" a vertical line, and then "Not Yet" a diagonal line. Depending on your question you will know if the answer is "Not Really" or "Not Yet".

In this pendulum language, the guides would not give a "Not Really" or "Not Yet" answer without first giving the answer "No". I would not see a diagonal line directly after a question.

....

That being said if you receive a diagonal answer without a "No" swing prior, stop and ask a validation question. Then ask if your guidance team is instructing you in a different way than this material. Go with what your personal team informs you.

....

If you're a beginner, and learning this language, expect to see a diagonal line only when following a "No" vertical line on the palm.

This command gives the guides an opportunity to answer a "No" to one of your questions in a different way, other than just saying "No." A "No" answer is very final and doesn't give room for the conversation to be expanded. "No" followed by "Not Really" or "Not Yet" communicates the answer you seek is not in the immediate future, but still has potential for change.

There are three purposes to the double negative. The first one is to invite more questions and conversations with your angelic team. The second reason is because the answer "No" is very sharp and final and that may not be the energy that the guides want to communicate. If you just receive the answer "No" it is very final. "No", "Not Yet", invites the lightworker to keep going with the inquiry. The third reason is the movement of the pendulum creates a rhythm and a flow. There is a connecting rhythm when the movement changes from vertical to diagonal. It changes the tone of the conversation. It keeps the energy of the conversation going with guides.

For example, you might want to know if you should move from your current home to a new location. You might ask, "Should I move to a new place?" You might receive the answer, "No", a vertical line, then the answer "Not Yet", a diagonal line. It could be the timing is off. A "Not Yet" response might prompt you to ask a further question. "Should I wait until I complete a specific goal? How long should I wait?" That might then prompt you to ask a number question. "How many days or months should I wait?" If you just received the answer "No", you may stop asking questions. The "No" "Not Really" answer inspires more questions. It's an indication that there is more information for you to receive.

You might be trying to decide if you should spend money on attending a workshop. Perhaps you are hesitant because it is expensive or you may already know some or most of the material. If you ask the question, "Is this a good workshop for me to attend?" you might get a "No", "Not Really" answer rather than a sharp, "No" answer. In this case, I would become curious as to why. Is the information not relevant? Is the workshop too expensive? Should I investigate a different program? When you get the "No" "Not Really" answer you are queued to ask another question.

Keeping the conversation going creates a current of energy flow. You can feel the current as the pendulum swing changes direction from vertical to diagonal. There is an emotional feeling behind the movement of the pendulum. The pendulum shift from vertical to diagonal validates that you are communicating with your spirit team. You are receiving more than a "No" answer, you are receiving feedback and an invitation from your team to ask another question. The command "No", "Not Yet" demonstrates this energy flow and keeps the dialog moving along.

....

**Practice the "Show Me" commands for Orientation to the 9 positions.
Practice the "Show Me" commands for "Yes", "No", "Not Really/Not Yet" before you move on.**

....

Not Ready to Tell You, No Comment

When I started to work with my guidance team I noticed that I would get a lot of counter-clockwise answers. I came to understand that counter-clockwise was the guides' way of saying, "We're Not Ready to Tell You," or "None of Your Business". In some cases it can mean, "Your Perspective on the Situation is Incorrect."

Often times the guides are not ready to tell you the information you seek. There are a number of reasons for this. The guides may honestly not know what outcome is in your highest best interest just yet. There may be karmic ties to relationships that you need to move through to resolve unfinished business.

Guides are always looking at potentials and probabilities. The reality of this timeline is creating itself in "real time". There are many possibilities which can affect the outcome. Sometimes we ask questions too far out in the future. Many occurrences can change a future outcome. They may be encouraging you to be more patient and see how your life unfolds. Often other people and situations also have to fall into place, and that has not yet occurred.

A counter-clockwise circle on the hand can also mean, "None of your business." Once we get the conversation flowing, we may start asking questions that are not directly affecting "our" personal outcome. This often happens if we start to ask gossip type questions. For example, "Is the guy I like interested in someone else?" This is an example of a third party question. A third party question is a question that is not related directly to you. Your spirit guide team is not on "his team".

Your guides are observing you, not him. Literally they would have to go to a member of the other person's angelic team and be allowed to seek the answer. This is not something your personal team will do, unless it is important for your personal growth. You will often get a counter-clockwise circle if you ask a question about a third party.

The guides prefer you ask relationship questions in regards to yourself. For example, a better question might be, "Should I have an attitude of non-attachment to this new boy that has not yet called me back?" You will probably get a "Yes" answer. You might be tempted to ask, "Will he call me back?" The pendulum might go back to counter-clockwise, meaning "wait and see", or "we are not ready to tell you."

Just because you have access to your guides, doesn't mean that your angelic team is going to give it all away. There needs to be some mystery in your life. If they don't want you to know, or feel it's a bad question, you see a counter-clockwise swing. Phrase your questions using an I-statement, the question should be about yourself.

If a conversation with your angelic team is occurring and the pendulum swing comes to a screeching halt, and all movement stops, this means "No Comment" or "Not Willing to Answer". The pendulum stops suspended at the center of your palm. It feels like there is a gravity at the center of the palm, holding the pendulum in place. This can be quite a dramatic movement. I learned that guides will be silent if they want us to do more research, feel like we asked an inappropriate question, or simply are not willing to give away the answer.

Diagram 6 on the hand chart shows, "no comment" or "not willing to answer". In this case, the pendulum comes to a complete stop, or still point. There is no movement at all. It can feel like the pendulum is anchored. The magnetic magic anchor will not let the pendulum swing until you ask another question.

I remember earlier in my career, I was asked by an internet radio show if I wanted to do a series on energy healing and chakras. I was so excited! I really wanted to do it, but it had a monetary investment associated with it. I was sure that it was a good avenue to try out. The idea got my heart pounding, my whole being said "Yes". I enthusiastically went to consult my guidance team. Clearly I was not going to make the investment without the enthusiastic "Yes" answer.

I remember going to my room, picking up the pendulum and enthusiastically asking, "Is this a good opportunity, should I move forward with this idea?" The pendulum just held at center. They didn't want to use the command "No". They simply replied "No Comment." My team didn't want hurt to my feelings, as I was so excited about the invitation. They decided to use the answer, "No comment" instead of a "No".

As I reflect on that experience, clearly, it was not the right time to make that career move. I got excited because the idea was part of my life purpose and I wanted to do this work. But I was not yet developed to the point where they wanted me to be teaching. I had not yet had my first psychic opening. I was ahead of myself and my projected timeline. In the moment,

I was disappointed, but now, as this book comes forward, it makes perfect sense. Sometimes the guides feel a "No" answer is too harsh, especially when you feel super excited about something or someone and can't understand the big picture.

Other times the pendulum stopped and moved to the still point because I asked a bad question, or someone on the team took offence to the question that I asked. I remember talking to an exalted "God" being. The entity was high up in dimensional hierarchy. We were having an exciting and interesting conversation about issues related to humanity. At the time, I was writing the **10 Cosmic Dimensions**. I was doing a lot of channeling on the deep subject of karma. This was before I became fully clairaudient. I wrote that book primarily using the pendulum as the communication device.

The pendulum was swinging away most of the day. Then I asked the question, "Shouldn't God apologize to humans for the world that he created?" I remember the pendulum came to a screeching halt. I felt bad. I thought, "Oh, I disrespected God." I remember hearing the message, "Go to the window, and look out." At that moment the most beautiful sunset I could imagine was cast over the horizon. Pink clouds lit up the sky as the sun went down over the sea. Our session was over. The pendulum didn't move till the next day.

Practice the "Show Me" commands for counter-clockwise, "Not Ready to Tell You" or "None of Your Business." Practice the "Show Me" command for "No Comment" and "Not Willing to Answer." Ask a few "Yes" and "No" questions that you know the answers to. Get the pendulum moving before you use the "Show Me" command for "Not Ready to Tell You".

First, ask a few "Yes" or "No" questions before you say "Show Me No Comment". This way you can understand how the pendulum halts and anchors to the center of the palm.

Certainly, Assign Names and Items to Your Fingers

Diagram 7 on the hand chart expresses the communication "Certainly", the pendulum swings to the right side of the palm (**position 6**). "Yes" and "Certainly" are both positive signals and close in meaning. "Certainly" is stronger than a "Yes". "Certainly" is more conversational and has a different tone. The answer you receive depends on your line of questioning and the feeling of enthusiasm your guides are trying to express to you.

Sometimes you will see the pendulum swing "Certainly" all by itself, but often times you will see the "Certainly" swing following the "Yes" answer. "Yes, Certainly" is a double positive, similar to the double negative of "No" followed by "Not Really".

There are three reasons why you might receive a double positive. The first one is to invite more questions and conversations with your angelic team. The second reason is because the answer "Yes" or "Certainly" or "Yes, Certainly" all have different tones of positive expression. In a conversation the positive momentum can build with these three different expressions of positive response. And finally there is an energy flow and rhythm that occurs when the pendulum moves from the clockwise circle to the middle of the inside palm. You can feel your angelic team is communicating and wants to keep the conversation going.

For example, you might ask, "Should I take time off of work and travel?" The guide responds, "Yes", then, "Certainly!" The guide's enthusiasm should prompt you to ask more questions. "How can I manifest this? How long will it take to raise the money? Should I just quit my job? What is the best timing for an adventurous trip?" If you get a "Yes", "Certainly" this should indicate to you to keep the conversation going.

I have noticed that when I am asking questions, I get "Yes", "Certainly" frequently. This command is more conversational then just a "Yes" answer and provides a strong enthusiastic encouragement. "Yes", "Certainly" means the same as "Two Thumbs Up" or "You're Definitely on the Right Track". It could also mean "Definitely Go", "Perform the Action" or "Take the Risk". The guides are certain you should do this activity.

There are many times in our journey when our insecurities or fears block our willingness to try something new or create an adventure for ourselves. The swing "Certainly" or "Yes, Certainly" encourages you to move out of your comfort zone. It communicates that you should definitely take the action, even if you feel you can't afford it or it is too uncomfortable for you. It's your guide's way of validating you in a way that is stronger than just a "Yes" answer. Ideas may start to come to you. You might start asking, "Do you mean this?" "Do you mean that?" If you keep getting "Certainly", it validates you. This creates more of a conversation with your guides.

You can expand the conversation and receive more information by assigning names or items to your fingers. For example, if you ask the question, "Is there a family member I should pay more attention to?" You can assign names to your fingers. Mom, could be your thumb (**finger 1**), auntie could be your pointer finger (**finger 2**), your older sister could be your middle finger (**finger 3**), and your younger brother could be your ring finger (**finger 4**), your pinky should be used for "Someone Else".

When assigning names and items to your fingers, it is important that the last finger is assigned to "Someone Else" or "Something Else". This leaves room to see if there is something else you may not have thought about. This is important because it prompts you to ask another question.

This technique is a great way to know which angelic guides you are talking to. After you know the names of your angels you can assign them a finger. You might want to know, "Which guide is working with me today?" Assign Sarah to finger one, Daniel to finger two, Jeremy to finger three and Steven to finger four. Assign finger five to "someone else". This creates a strong relationship with your angelic team. It allows you to know who you are communicating with. When I look back at my journals and notes, I always wrote down who was communicating to me on different topics. This is a way to build a strong relationship with your team.

If your intention is to communicate with your angelic team and you get the answer, "someone else", don't panic. Remember, spirit communication can be tricky. We are working with the invisible realm and many environments are not clear.

If the pendulum moves to your pinky finger, I would ask another series of questions. Is this a guide (**finger 1**), an angel (**finger 2**), a lost soul (**finger 3**), a negative energy (**finger 4**) or something else (**finger 5**)? Many times I found the communication was coming from a lost soul fragment that wanted to be crossed over, rather than a guide. In this case, I would meditate and ask my guidance team to cross them over to the other side. If it is a negative energy, then it needs to be cleared, you can't trust the answers to the questions you seek.

Using this technique, I learned a lot of information. I remember waking up in the morning knowing that I astral-traveled. I would sit up and meditate for a few moments, pull out the pendulum and ask, "Where did I travel to last night in dreamtime?" Did I go to the Light Realms (**finger 1**), did I meet galactics (**finger 2**), did I travel on the Earth plane (finger 3), or something else (**finger 4**)? If I got finger 1 for the Light Realms I would ask, "What did I do there last night?" Meet with my guides (**finger 1**), participate in a class (**finger 2**), meet someone new (**finger 3**), go to a different astral plane (**finger 4**) or something else (**finger 5**).

I would wait to see where the pendulum swung and then use my clairvoyant skills to see if I got a vision that would come to me. I would let my mind relax and intend to see clairvoyantly. Several times I remember receiving the answer that I met with galactics. I would close my eyes and focus at the point between the eyebrows. I would remember walking around on a large ship with a group of people looking out of the window of a galactic ship.

I would continue with another line of questioning. "What did I do on the ship?" Was I learning something (**finger 1**)? Was I on a mothership (**finger 2**)? Were there other humans on the ship (**finger 3**)? Was there an Ascended Master on the ship (**finger 4**)? In this way I discovered many interesting entities and places in the 5th dimension and beyond. Once you understand how to assign your fingers to have different names and items, you can get very creative in your questioning.

....

Practice the "Show Me" commands for "Certainly". Next practice the "Show Me" commands for the five fingers. Assign your angel names to your fingers, assign family member names or other items for topics that interest you. Have fun!

....

Scaling Questions

As time was progressing, I was starting to develop more ways of asking questions to gather information. Coming from a psychology background, I had the idea to ask scaling questions to find out if my angelic team thought I would benefit from events, working with spiritual teachers or purchasing products. Over time the scaling questions expanded. I could get feedback on nearly everything I wanted to know.

To this day, when clients come for a reading, I use the scaling method when contacting my client's angelic team to get feedback on any number of questions. The scale is from 1 to 6. Your five fingers are numbered one to five, and the 6th is on the right side of the middle palm. Diagram 9 shows Position 6.

The scale from 1 to 6 is as follows. The thumb (**finger 1**), means don't do it. The pointer finger (**finger 2**), means not recommended. The middle finger (**finger 3**) means neutral. Neutral means you can take it or leave it. It's something you could do and would not harm you, although, it's not extremely beneficial either. The ring finger (**finger 4**), means some benefit would be received. The pinky finger (**finger 5**), means what you are asking about is beneficial. The 6 position to the inside middle of the palm means, "Very Beneficial, Definitely Do It!"

If you get a 4 or 5 on the scaling question, I normally recommend that the client takes the action they are asking about. Obviously if you get a 6, your angelic team definitely feels the action is highly beneficial, and you should go for it. Likewise, I would not recommend taking an action if you get a 1 or 2. This simple scaling question has guided my path over the years.

Later I had the idea that I wanted to check out my physical body systems. I pulled out an anatomy diagram. I went through all the systems of my body and all of my organs. I wanted to know which organs might be weaker. I could start taking supplements or reconsider food choices. I checked out all my body systems: circulatory, digestive, endocrine, integumentary, lymphatic, muscular, nervous, reproductive, respiratory and skeletal. I decided to ask the scaling questions for organs. I asked about my liver, my intestine, my heart and my brain all on a scale from 1 to 6.

The interpretation of the scaling questions for the physical body is the following. Finger 1, means you are suffering from an illness. If you get a 1, you would know through physical pain that you are suffering in that area of the body. Finger 2 means the body part, body system or organ is declining in health. You should take precautions or see a doctor regarding your concern. Finger 3 means you are in satisfactory condition with no immediate concerns, but could improve that area of the body with supplements or changes in diet. Finger 4 means that body part is healthy and finger 5 means the body is very healthy. Finger 6 means you are at an optimal health for that organ or body system.

For example, I knew I had weak kidneys based on my family history. My left kidney is at a 3 and my right kidney is at a 4. This was my weakest organ. To this day, I watch my sugar intake carefully. If my kidneys decline to a 2, I would be at risk for getting diabetes. If I got a 1, then I would be suffering with diabetes. In this way, you can ask scaling questions to discover information about your own health. You may also receive information about others, if you are advancing as a reader and have their permission to inquire about this information.

You can ask a broad range of questions with scaling questions. It's fun and exciting to get such powerful and instant feedback from your angelic team. And again, a cautionary note. If the answers don't seem right, or it goes against your common sense, go back and ask the validation questions. Obviously if you get a number 1 for illness on a body part that you know is healthy, you are most likely experiencing interference.

Practice the "Show Me" commands for scaling questions. Ask some scaling questions 1 to 6 for questions you know the answers to. Then move to questions you are inquiring about.

Numbers on the Hand

As time moved on, I had a need to retrieve numbers faster than pulling numbers off of a chart to get the information. Numbers 1 to 5 are obviously our fingers numbered 1 to 5. But I wanted a quick way to get to 10. I decided that each finger should represent two numbers. 1 through 5 and 6 through 10.

I would ask for the number between 1 and 10. If the swing of the pendulum was to the ring finger (**finger 4**), I would know the answer would be either 4 or 9. Then I asked, "Is the number 4 or 9?" If the pendulum swung to the thumb (**finger 1**) it would be 4. If the pendulum swung to the pointer finger (**finger 2**) the answer was 9. I practiced this way for a long time, to find out numbers 1 to 10 quickly.

As my psychic development continued to advance, my clairsentient skill improved. Over time, the pendulum would swing to the ring finger (**finger 4**) and I would just know the correct answer was 9. Again, remember, the pendulum is meant to be training wheels for developing clairaudience or clairsentience. When clairaudience occurs you hear the answer, when clairsentience occurs you know the answer intuitively. As your intuition develops, you hear or know the answer before the pendulum swing reveals the answer. You know your psychic skills are improving.

Another question along these same lines are percentage questions. I found I could get percentage answers in much the same fashion. For example, "What percentage of humanity are lightworkers or advanced souls currently on the planet?" The answer comes, "About 30% of the human population are advanced souls." When I ask the question, "What percentage of the advanced souls are awake and conscious of who they are?" I get the answer, today in 2019, "About 7% are aware they are lightworkers."

When I ask the question, "Of these 7%, what percentage are aware of their life purpose and mission?" I get the answer about 4% are working hard on their lightworker missions. When I ask the question, "What percentage of the lightworkers are in the ascension process and starting to awaken?" I get the answer about 40% are actively waking up and coming online to perform their missions. You can see from this line of questioning that in 2019 we are still early in the ascension process.

Another way to ask forecasting questions is by using this % question: Is this concern 50% likely to occur or 50% unlikely to occur. Even though I have a direct connection with my angelic team, I never thought of myself as a fortune teller. I thought of myself as a healer and a spiritual counselor. I felt very uncomfortable when people asked me questions about their future. I knew this was not my mission, and further, my team was very clear to me, the future is not set in stone.

Life is a winding road. I was taught by my angelic team to think of the future as holding potentials and the probability of things to come. They taught me to ask the question, "Is this 50% likely to occur or 50% unlikely to occur?" That addressed the potential for something to happen, rather than saying, "Yes, this is something that is definitely going to happen to you" or "No, that is not likely to happen to you".

If the answer is 50% likely to occur, then allow for events to unfold and be optimistic. If you receive the answer that something is 50% likely not to occur, then you should let it go and not be attached. I use my thumb (**finger 1**) for 50% likely to occur and my pinky (**finger 5**) for 50% not likely to occur.

When you use a number chart to gather information about numbers, you can use the bottom arch to find out how many digits are in the number answer you were looking for. Use the "digit question" when you know the answer is over 10. The thumb means the digit is in the ones place, the pointer finger means the digit is in the tenths place and the middle finger means the digit is in the hundredths place.

That being said, I would suggest using the number chart, rather than your hand, if you are trying to receive information for numbers larger than 10. If you receive a counter-clockwise swing when asking a number question, that means the number is larger than 10, or you need to change the way you are asking the question.

Practice the "Show Me" commands for finding numbers from 1 to 10. Ask your guides to pick a number for you. Allow the pendulum to move to the correct finger. Then ask if it is the first number or the second number. Next, practice the 50% likely or unlikely command. Say out loud, "Show Me 50% Likely to Occur" and "50% Not Likely to Occur". Make sure you use questions you know the answers to and validate the spin. Then ask a few questions you are curious about.

Time Marks on the Hand

One of the most important questions in this work is, "Am I clear enough to channel?" This is one of the validation questions. If you receive the answer "No", you are likely experiencing interference and cannot trust the answers. The next question should be, "How long should I clear myself and meditate before I attempt to channel?" This question prompted me to start assigning minutes to my fingers.

Early on, I might receive an answer, "twenty minutes". I would go to my meditation corner, do my clearing exercises for a few minutes, then meditate for a total of twenty minutes. After that process, I would ask again, "Am I clear enough to channel?" If I got a "Yes", I would move forward with my divination tools seeking guidance from my angelic team.

If you are unclear about the differences between clearing and meditation, please refer to the **100 Chakra System** book where this topic is discussed at length. To quickly summarize, "clearing" refers to clearing the energy body, which contains our chakra system numbering up to 100 or more and our outer auric field. Meditation refers to expanding the Lightbody, the soulful body, and feeling love and oneness with all that is.

There are different ways you can clear the energy body. The easiest way is to hold the intention of clearing the chakras and ask your personal team to assist you in the clearing process while you sit still. You can also listen to a chakra-clearing meditation, there are several on my YouTube channel. After your energy body is clear and you feel more settled and balanced, you are ready to channel or meditate.

Diagram 11 shows time marks for minutes, in five minute intervals. The thumb (**finger 1**) means 5 minutes, the pointer finger (**finger 2**) means 10 minutes, the middle finger (**finger 3**) means 15 minutes, the right finger (**finger 4**) means 20 mins and the pinky finger (**finger 5**) means 25 mins. You can use the 6th position at the right side middle of the palm to mean 30 minutes. Program your left hand now for time marks as they pertain to minutes. I use this measure primarily for the question, "How long should I clear the energy body to be clear enough to channel?"

Diagram 12 shows the time mark for length of time in terms of days, weeks, months and years. This is helpful when we want to project future outcomes. One could ask the question, "When is this transition in my life going to complete itself?" If the pendulum swings to the middle finger, the answer would be months. You might then ask, "How many months?" And then use the finger on the hand to get more information.

Let's say the pendulum went to the third finger meaning months of time. Then you ask for the number of months and you get "3", meaning three months of time. You might notice the pendulum continues to swing to position "6", meaning six months of time. Whenever I ask a question about length of time, my guides taught me the answer comes in a range of time. Depending on your question, you may just get one number, but if you are asking about a transitionary period, you are likely to get two numbers to create the range of time. In this example, the transition will complete itself in three to six months of time.

You could also ask for the range of the transitionary time, and channel in two numbers to give you a projected timeframe. When we are moving locations, changing jobs or facing changes in a relationship there is always a transition during which we adjust to our new set of circumstances. I know from being a therapist that transitions always take longer than one thinks they should. This is one reason why the guides give a range rather than a hard, set in stone time.

If the pendulum swings to the pinky finger (**finger 5**) this means, "Not Enough Information Keep Researching." This can happen when the guides can't tell you the answer you seek. This comes up a lot when people are wondering about their life story too far out in the future. Often times there are many potentials and people and events have to fall into place before your path is clearly known.

Forecasting questions are likely to be more accurate if you search about three months out or less into the future. The truth is a lot of potentials and synchronicities can occur at any moment which can change your plans or ideas about the future. As a therapist I have watched people move through their stories. They might feel certain about wanting something to occur only to find there is another event that comes up. The event is a better situation, or gives them pause to make other considerations.

The other reason you might get the response "Not Enough Info Keep Researching", is there are other avenues of possibilities that you need to review or discover.

Something has not yet occurred to you. People go to a therapist looking to find new insights about what direction to take. Many times clients have come to me seeking a new vocation and more meaningful work. A counselor or coach with different insight can give you new ideas, or change your perspective. This is the guides' way of saying, "We understand you want your answer, but you haven't looked at all the potential. Keep researching." Researching could mean finding a therapist or coach to give you feedback and a new perspective.

Practice the "Show Me" commands for finding time marks. Say out loud, "Show Me", "5", "10", "15", "20", "25" and "30".

Next, say out loud, "Show Me Days", "Show Me Weeks", continue through the fingers. Ask how many minutes you need to meditate each day and how many days per week. Make the questions conversational.

Sit to meditate with the intention of clearing your energy body for 5 to 10 minutes.

Use the pendulum on hand to ask, "Am I Clear Enough to Channel?"
- **If you get a "Yes"** answer then start asking your questions.
- **If you get a "No"** answer you are holding negative energy from your daily experience and are likely to receive interference.

Ask how long you should sit to meditate to clear your energy body.

Let your guides inform you how long you should meditate to be clear enough to channel.

Number your fingers for Time Marks for Minutes, shown on **Diagram 11 on page 57** to receive your answer.

If you receive a counter-clockwise swing or continue to receive a "No" answer after meditation, then you may need to do some clearing work in the Higher Chakras and Ascending Chakras prior to working with the pendulum tool.

Refer to the book **The 100 Chakra System** for more information on clearing the Higher Chakras and Ascending Chakras.

"Am I Clear Enough to Channel" is the most important validation question.

PENDULUM ON THE HAND

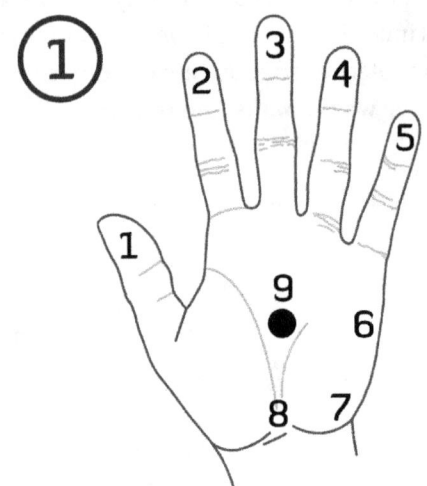

ORIENTATION

LEFT HAND PALM UPRIGHT
FINGERS NUMBERED 1-10

6 - Right Side Middle of Palm
7 - Right Corner of Palm
8 - Center of Wrist
9 - Center of Palm

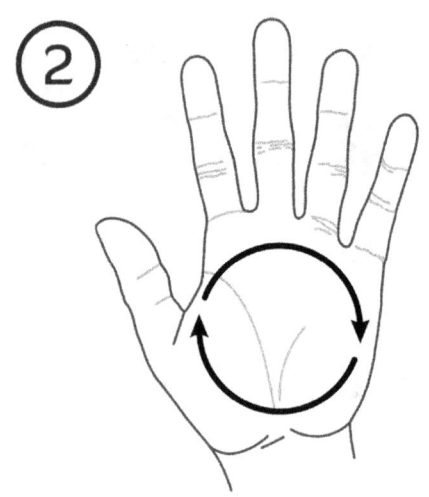

YES

CLOCKWISE

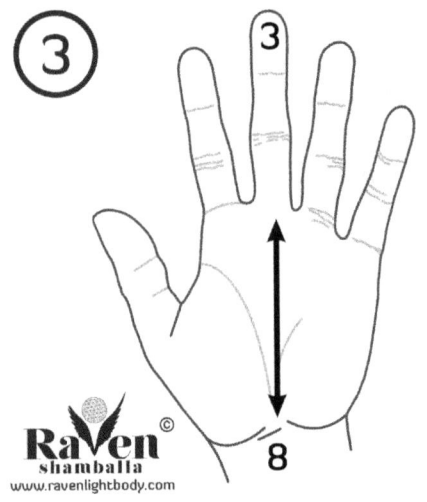

NO

VERTICAL LINE

3rd Finger to Center of Wrist

PENDULUM ON THE HAND

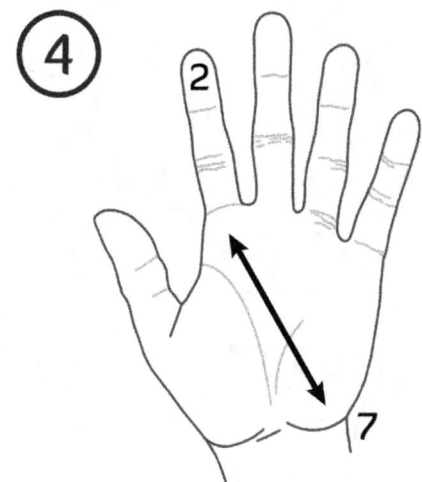

④ NOT REALLY
NOT YET

DIAGONAL LINE

2nd Finger to Right Side Corner of Palm

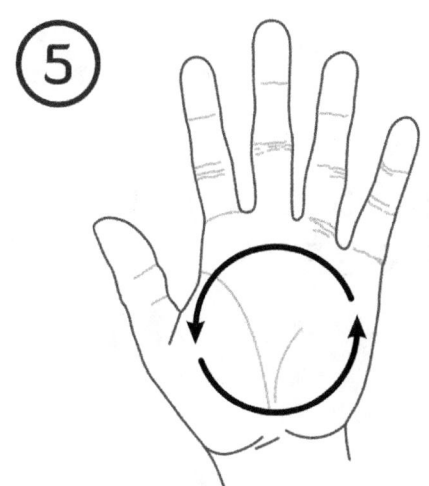

⑤ NOT READY TO TELL YOU
NONE OF YOUR BUSINESS

COUNTER-CLOCKWISE

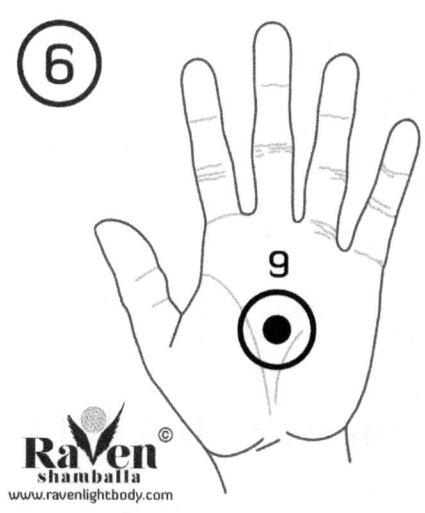

⑥ NO COMMENT
NOT WILLING TO ANSWER

**STILL POINT
NO MOVEMENT**

Center of Palm

PENDULUM ON THE HAND

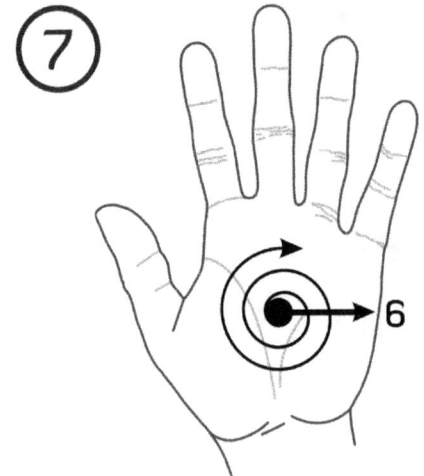

CERTAINLY
POSITION 6

DEFINITELY
PENDULUM SWINGS UP

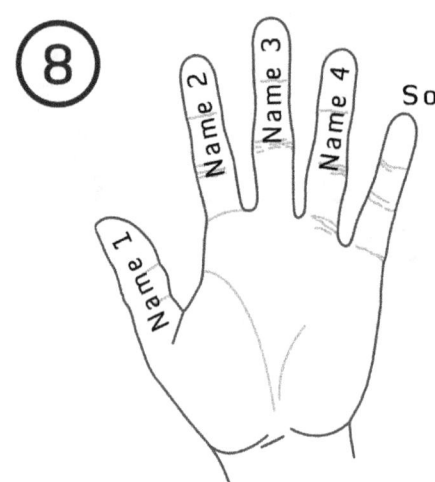

Something Else

ASSIGN NAMES OR ITEMS TO YOUR FINGERS
POSITION 7

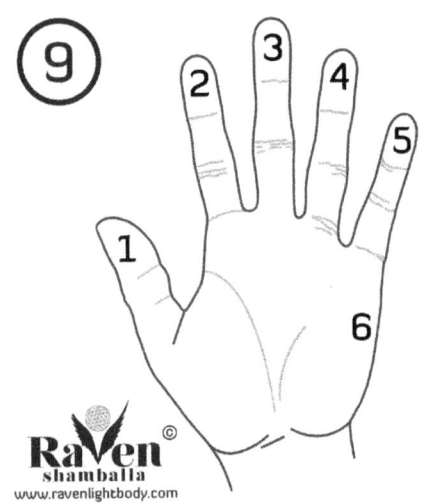

SCALING 1 TO 6

1 - Don't Do
2 - Not Recommended
3 - Neutral
4 - Some Benefit
5 - Beneficial
6 - Definitely Beneficial DO IT!

PENDULUM ON THE HAND

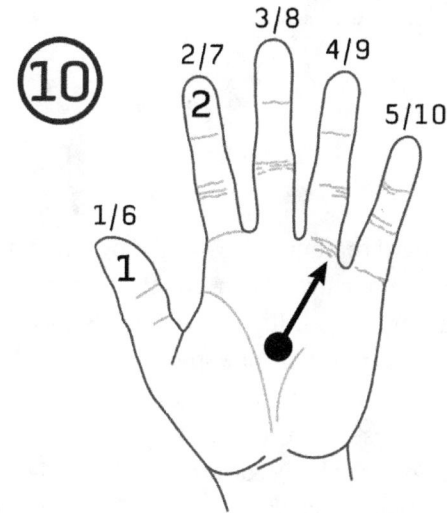

NUMBERS
(see hand for numbers)

Example Swing can be 4 or 9

1 - First Number
2 - Second Number

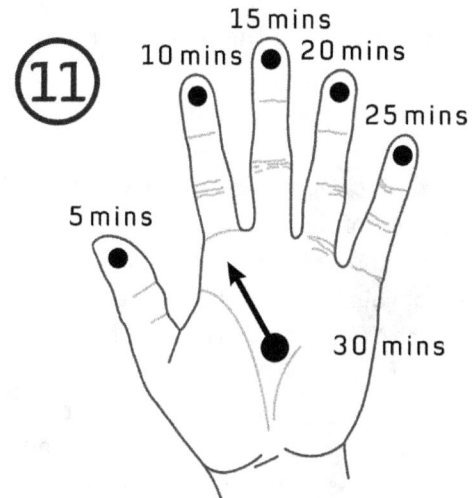

TIME MARKS
MINUTES
(see hand for minutes)

Example Swing 10 Minutes

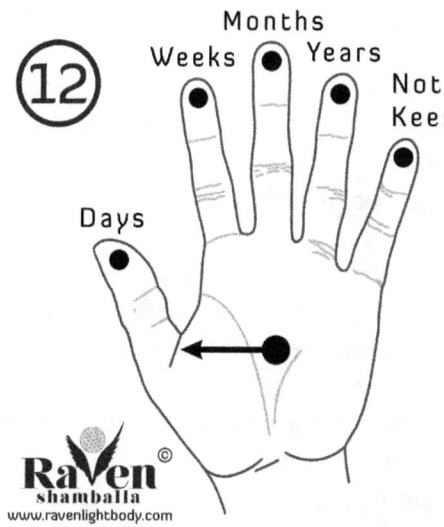

TIME MARKS
LENGTH OF TIME
(see hand for time mark)

Example Swing Days to Event

Chapter 8. Making Conversation with your Angelic Team

Guides Want Us to Take the Lead

As I have taught people how to use their pendulum to make contact with their angelic team, one of the questions I've received is, "What kinds of questions do I ask my guides?" The other comment is that people tend to ask questions incorrectly and just get counter-clockwise, for "Not Ready to Tell You" or in some cases it can mean, "Inappropriate Question". Chapter 8 and Chapter 9 help to address that question.

When I started the work of asking very detailed questions, my guides were rather surprised. They let me know they were not used to this level of detailed communication and correspondence. The fact that many humans can channel and work more directly with their guides is because of the "Ascension Process". Ascension means that humans are now evolving and are more conscious and aware of the 5th dimension and higher dimensional realms. As a result, the veils are lifting between the two dimensions and we have more contact with the other side.

At the same time, the guides are also getting used to the veils being lifted. The guides are not used to having such direct communication with humans. If you look at the traditional charts, there were only a few words, "Yes, No, Maybe and Rephrase." Pendulum on the hand is taught to be conversational. One question leads to another question, which leads to another question.

Once I knew who was in the room working with me, I felt like I knew them as friends that I conversed with often. The relationship became very relaxed. I asked many questions, I complained when things didn't go my way. I would want to know why they didn't inform me of something. I asked hard questions and demanded to know who was making decisions.

I complained when I felt more challenged than I imagined. And of course, I had the classic and most often asked question, "How do I get the money to manifest this mission?" "How do I fulfill my 3rd dimensional obligations and also my deepest desires to do good in the world?"

For us, it is hard to understand why movement and change happen in our lives. What I realize is you have to trust in the story of your life as it unfolds. Sometimes I felt like the guides would hold up a sign saying, "We refuse the right to answer all your questions." or, "There still needs to be mystery in the search."

I remember, one time, I needed to find a new place to live. I remember the conversation going something like, "Can't you guys just tell me which apartment I should move into? I know you know the answer, won't you just tell me?"

I was looking for an apartment in the area and they asked me to go out and do a diligent search. When I returned, I asked which apartment would work best. "The answer came, "None of these, an apartment will not suit your needs in the future." Well that was three hours of my life I was not going to get back. "Why did you make me do that search?" They answered, "To eliminate those choices from your potentials".

About a week later I got an intuitive hit to check the listings now. I went to a website that I had not searched yet. There was a townhouse in my price range. That was the one, I knew it! I asked and the response came, "Yes, apply." I moved into the townhouse and it was the only place I needed to apply for. I hadn't imaged I could find a home with a two-car garage in my price range. The guides knew where I was going to live, prior to me.

They decided not to point to the answer, but required that I move through the life process of searching and exploring the answer for myself. My spirit guides preferred I go through the experience of searching for the answer. They expanded my vision about what might occur and eliminated choices that they knew were not in my highest best interest. Even though I had a close relationship and daily communication, the answer came in Divine timing. I was still required to move through the discovery process.

Using the Pendulum Conversation Style

The purpose of learning the pendulum language on the hand is that you can create a conversation. This is very different communication than just asking "Yes" or "No" questions. Once you can get the pendulum to swing, the pendulum moves in a way which allows for a conversation. It's like using an old-fashioned telegraph that you might see in an old movie. The telegraph was used in the 1840's prior to the telephone. The communication device revolutionized long-distance communication by transmitting electrical signals over the wire between two stations. One person would tap out a message that could be received across a long distance.

You can use the pendulum as a communication device. Once you get the conversation started, the pendulum moves swiftly. Guides will use the "Yes" and "No" signals followed by double negatives, or double positives. If you keep asking questions, it's like phoning to the 5th dimension and using an instrument to ask different kinds of questions.

I am often asked, "What kind of questions do I ask my guides?"

If you are focused on general life path questions about life purpose, career and relationships, you can often run out of topics to converse about. Life Path questions are important questions and of course, our most pressing concerns. We should ask about our deepest concern. But life path questions should be asked occasionally. Often, time just has to pass before we know the outcome.

Guides prefer we have fun asking questions. They like when we ask about health and healing. Guides like to be asked questions about metaphysical topics. It's fun to dive into the mystery of the universe. The idea is to have fun with the work and create a conversation when speaking with your angelic team.

By linking together questions, you can create a dialog. When this starts to happen, it makes the process of spirit communication very real and tangible. You know that you are not moving the pendulum, and you are getting quick and rapid responses. You don't have to pull out different charts to get the information, you can just move from one question to the next. The conversation becomes fluid.

Feeling for the Conversation

From the tone of the following conversations, you can see how the energy of the answer is neutral, or starts to become positive or negative. You can see that the guides are in the role of counselor, rather than telling you what to do. They are assisting you in listening to yourself to help you find the best solution. You can also see that research is required. Once you have some items to look at, the guides can give you feedback.

There is a certain amount of "feeling for the conversation". This is similar to using your intuition to feel through a situation. As you practice you start to know what the guides are trying to communicate to you. You also start to understand if they are willing to answer that type of question, or if they feel like you are relying too much on them for the answers.

The following pages contain four example conversations. The conversations are brief and designed to give you an idea of how you might move from question to question to create a dynamic conversation. The examples allow you to feel for the tone of the conversation to give you an idea of "feeling for the conversation".

Example Conversation 1. Should I go back to school?

Perform the validation questions and make sure you are clear enough to channel.

Q. What is the name of the Angel or Guide that is assisting me today? (**Assign names to fingers**)
A. Sarah (**finger 1**).

Q. Hello Sarah, many blessings to you today. I felt bored again at work today. I like my job, but wonder, is it time for me to go back to school?
A. Yes. (**clockwise circle**) Certainly! (**position 6**)

Q. What kind of education is best for me at this point in my life?
A formal education (**finger 1**), a certification (**finger 2**), a healing workshop (**finger 3**) or something else (**finger 4**).
A. A formal education (**finger 1**)

Q. Hum...that seems hard to me and expensive.
A. No (**vertical line**), Not Really (**diagonal line**)

Q. If I were to go back, what college majors should I pursue? **Do a quick internet search for five college majors you have thought about trying.** On a scale from 1 to 6, which of these college majors should I pursue?
A. Nursing (**scores a 4**), Environmental Studies (**scores a 2**), Business (**scores a 4**), Counseling (**scores a 5**)

Q. I feel fearful about the cost of the investment, is this the right direction for me?
A. Yes (**clockwise**) Certainly (**position 6**)

Q. I am just not sure how I feel about it. Could I wait to go to school?
A. Yes. (**clockwise**)

Q. How much longer should I stay in my current position? (**length of time**)
A. Months (**finger 3**)

Q. How many months, give me a range (**numbers on hand**)
A. 1 to 3 months (**finger 1, then finger 3**)
Q. That is not very long, do you want me to move soon?
A. Yes! Definitely! (**clockwise, then pendulum swings up**)

Q. Should I go to school this spring, or wait till fall for the beginning of the school year? (**assign finger 1 - Fall, assign finger 2 - Spring**)
A. Spring (**finger 2**), (**clockwise, then pendulum swings up**)

In this conversation, you can tell the person asking the questions has a lot of fear and uncertainty about making a decision about how to advance their career and if school is a good idea or not. The guides are very forward about encouraging her to go back to school.

The conversation requires her to do some research to ask the guides about it. She asks about what majors to choose and scoring them. The guidance she received is for her to go back to school very soon and not delay on creating new potentials in her future. There is a lot of energy coming from her team encouraging her to move forward.

Example Conversation 2. What workshop should I take?

Perform the validation questions and make sure you are clear enough to channel.

Q. What guide am I speaking with today? (**assign names to fingers**)
A. Daniel (**finger 2**)

Q. I feel like I want to take a workshop to enrich my yoga practice, but I am not sure if I should take an internet class, go to a yoga workshop, or do a formal Level 2 training. Maybe I should train in a different style of yoga altogether. (**assign items to fingers, finger 5 – is something else**)
A. Something else (**finger 5**)

Q. Humm. What else would assist my spiritual practice at this time? Do a quick search online. Search Different Types of Yoga. (**assign yoga styles to fingers – finger 5 is something else**)
A. Something Else (**finger 5**)

Q. Humm. I don't know? Ask a validation question. Is this Daniel, my guide?
A. Yes, Certainly (**clockwise, position 6**)

Q. Should I look at other topics that complement yoga?
A. Yes, Certainly (**clockwise, position 6**)

Q. Maybe I should study meditation, chanting, yoga philosophy, hypnosis, crystals (**assign finger – position 6 means something else**)
A. Chanting (**finger 2**)

Q. Chanting? I don't really sing or know how to speak in Sanskrit.
A. No Comment (**pendulum halts to still point**)

Q. You want me to try something new?
A. Yes. Certainly! (**clockwise circle to position 6**)

Humm...

....

Take a moment to think about it, do some research, look to see if there are any workshops for chanting near your location. You find a chanting workshop. An out-of-town guest is coming to visit a nearby yoga studio!

....

Q. Is this the workshop that I should attend?
A. Yes Definitely. (**clockwise circle then pendulum swings up**)

Q. Ok Daniel, I will try it out. Thank you!

In the second example, there was an avenue that the person was overlooking. The guidance was to look outside of the box and try something new. Notice how important the "Something Else" question was in the process of this person expanding their options. The person started the conversation on the topic of investigating styles of yoga and ended up in a different, yet related category of singing and chanting.

Through asking questions, the person asking found a workshop they were not yet considering. Guides love to do this. This is one of the guides' purposes, to expand your horizons and point you in directions you may not have considered. Who knows, maybe there is a new friend waiting for you to be discovered that you end up meeting at that workshop. After the fact, you might say to your guides, "So that's why you wanted me to go. I learned new information and met a new friend."

Example Conversation 3. What happened last night in dreamtime?

After you wake up in the morning, sit to meditate. Ask the validation questions.

Q. Good morning. What guide am I speaking with today? (**assign names to fingers**)
A. Philip (**finger 3**)

Q. I feel like I traveled last night in Dreamtime. I also know I had an interesting dream. Did my etheric body travel last night?
A. Yes (**clockwise circle**)

Q. Where did I go? (**assign items to fingers**) The Light Realms/Heaven (**finger 1**), To Meet a Galactic (**finger 2**), To Other Astral Planes (**finger 3**)? Or Somewhere Else (**finger 4**)?
A. To Other Astral Planes (**finger 3**)

Q. I remember something about a water world. **Meditate for a few minutes and see if any images come to you.** I remember swimming with dolphins. I remember hearing their high-pitched sound.
A. Yes. (**clockwise**) Certainly (**position 6**)

Q. What was I doing there? (**assign items to fingers**) Working on a Project (**finger 1**), Meeting with Someone Important (**finger 2**), Relaxing (**finger 3**), or Something Else (**finger 4**)?
A. Meeting with Someone Important (**finger 2**) then (**counter clockwise**)

Q. I don't understand the counter-clockwise?
A. No Comment (**pendulum halts at center of palm**)

Q. Meeting with someone, maybe the "important" is not correct.
A. Yes

Q. Meeting with my soul family (**finger 1**), Meeting with a guide (**finger 2**) Meeting with an astral friend (**finger 3**) or Something else (**finger 4**).
A. Meeting with my soul family (finger 1).

Q. Is there an aspect of me that is from a water world on a higher dimension?
A. Yes (**clockwise**) Definitely (**pendulum swings up**). Ask more questions about your soul family – Male or Female, Types of Relationship, Have you known them before? When?

Q. That is really interesting. I feel like I'm at one with the mermaids. When I swim in the ocean, I feel very free. **Take some time to meditate and see if anything comes to you.**

Q. I have a feeling like I should go swimming today! I want to feel free. I had another vision of walking on the beach shore. I feel like I was in the water and then I came to the shore. Was that part of traveling in dreamtime?
A. No (**vertical line**) Not Really (**diagonal line**).

Q. Maybe that is more about me and what I should do today.
A. Yes. (**clockwise**)

Q. It's Saturday, I think I will call friends and plan a trip to the water. Yes, that is what I will do.

The third conversation is meant to give ideas for asking metaphysical questions. You can ask all kinds of questions. What did the dream mean? If you are reading a book, you can ask if your guides agree or disagree with the author's concept. Is there life on other planets? You can have a lot of fun traveling into different dimensions through these conversations. In this example, the person stops to meditate and practice seeing clairvoyantly. It's a combination of using the pendulum, seeing clairvoyantly, using your intuition and having fun in the exploration. This line of questions will advance you quickly.

Notice how the person asking the question states, "I don't understand what counter-clockwise means?" She thinks about it, and then rephrases the question. Notice that what happens in dreamtime and how it directs the course of his day off.

Example Conversation 4. What vitamins or supplements should I take?

A friend has told you about some great new line of products that are for health and healing. You are wondering if your guides think that you should purchase these products or not. Sit to meditate and then ask the validation questions.

Q. What guide am I speaking with this evening? **(assign names to fingers)**
A. Sarah **(finger 1)**

Q. Thank you for coming to speak with me. I am always blessed by your presence. I wanted to ask you some questions about these new health and healing products. I am wondering if I should purchase them and which ones would be best for me. Here are the products that I am interested in. I will let you review the ingredients. **Look over the ingredient list.**

Which products should I purchase? Should I Assign Items to Fingers **(finger 1)** or Make a List **finger 2)**.

A. Make a List **(finger 2)**

Q. But there are so many great products, I know I can't afford them all. I will run the pendulum over the items in the catalog. If you think my body needs them, make a circle, ok?
A. Yes **(clockwise circle)** or Certainly **(position 6)**.

Q. **Hold the pendulum over the catalog items, if you get a yes write it down or mark it. Imagine out of 20 products you are interested in, 9 products get a circle for "Yes".**

Great, thank you, that narrows it down. Let's scale the items so I know which one my body needs the most.

A. Yes **(clockwise circle)** or Certainly **(position 6)**.

Q. On a Scale from 1 to 6, what is the first product?
A. You get 4.

Q. **Continue to scale the 9 products.**
A. Product 2: 3, Product 3: 5...**(keep going)**, Product 8: 6, Product 9: 5.

Q. 4 of the products scaled 5 and 1 of the products scaled a 6.

I will get the 6 product for sure. But what about the other 4?

A. Not Going to Tell You/ or in this case, Make Up Your Own Mind **(counter-clockwise)**

Q. I guess I will check my budget and see what I can afford? They all sound like they would be good for my body.
A. Yes **(clockwise)** Definitely! **(pendulum swings up)**

The last discussion gives you an example of how you might use the guide's feedback to assist you in narrowing down items and then scaling them. You still are required to do the research and bring items forward to be considered. In this conversation, the angel is willing to help narrow down the list, but then holds back about how many items to buy or how much money to spend. You are still in the driver's seat and you have received guidance, but not the exact answers about which one to buy.

Free Will and Choice

Be very cautious if the pendulum starts telling you what to do. I know from experience, this is not how the white light guides behave. Your angels will not make decisions for you. They want you to be the responsible party. You are currently incarnate as a humanoid on Earth which is a free will and choice zone. If the pendulum feels like it is being demanding, or telling you what actions to take, step back. Ask the validation questions. If you start to feel like you just don't know if you can trust the pendulum, put it down. Go back to using your intuition without it.

Remember the pendulum is only a spiritual tool. Your ultimate goal should be intuition and feeling the development of psychic abilities. At times put the pendulum down and use your intuition skills to feel for the answer without using the pendulum. The "hand to heart chakra method" offers a good technique for advancing intuition. Place your dominant hand on your heart chakra. Ask a question. If you get a warm and excited feeling, do that! If you feel down about it, or unsure, don't do that. It's is good old-fashioned feeling that helps to develop clairsentience, the ability to just know, or know by feeling.

Ultimately we need to own our decisions and actions. We have incarnated to make a difference on the Earth. The guides in the 5th dimension are like coaches, they can give up plays to run the ball, they can offer motivation and they are invested in you winning the game; but ultimately you incarnated as the athlete. You are on the field, you are in real-time on the Earth and you are the only one that can score a touchdown.

The guides want to offer assistance and guidance, but ultimately it's up to you and you have free will and choice. From this perspective, be aware if you are being told what to do or if you are asked to take actions that don't feel right to you. If this starts to happen, or you are concerned about your guidance, asked the validation questions and make sure who is corresponding with you. If in doubt, seek out a professional psychic teacher that is further along on the spiritual path.

Feeling for Your Guides

Another technique you should practice is feeling for the energy of your angels and spirit guides. They have personality and vibrations. When working with your guides you can feel for their personalities or feel for their presence in your auric field. There is a sense that you are not alone. Once the pendulum is moving, you know the guide is in your auric field or in a chakra center. It is important to stop and feel for their energy and personality.

This is one way a lightworker can develop clairsentience, the ability to feel or know. At times in your communication practice, close your eyes and feel for the personalities of your angelic team, especially if they have named themselves to you. Are they stern and serious or nurturing and lighthearted? Do they feel male, female or neither? Feeling for your team is another communication and relationship tool. You can start to recognize the different personalities through feelings. This is helpful for companionship and also being able to intuitively know who you are working with.

These brief conversations show how you can use questioning to create conversation and develop your relationship with your angelic team. For more examples of conversations with the pendulum, search 'Raven Shamballa and Pendulum' on YouTube or participate in a workshop with Raven.

Chapter 9.   What Kind of Questions Should I Ask?

Life Path Questions

Several times in my career, I will hear questions like: "I want to know what my guides want me to do, and then I will just do that." I respond, "Well, the guides want to know what you want to do, and they will assist you to get there." This is called co-creating with your angelic team. There is discussion and feedback. There are considerations along the journey. You may change your mind about what you want to develop. Or a consequence may come in that produces a situation you were not intending.

Guides are not in the business of telling us what to do, or defining our life for us. They are in the role of guidance, we still have free will and choice. Sometimes we have to take two steps back to move one step forward. For example, when you leave a long-term relationship it's hard to start over, it may feel like you took two steps back. But once you are free, doorways and opportunities are available to open. Often the guides are waiting for us to take a step in the direction of doing something different, which creates an opportunity for them to create a change.

From a guidance perspective, life purpose goals are often generalized. For example, one time a person came for a session. She had just graduated with a master's degree and wanted to know what direction to take in life. Her guides responded, "Your life purpose is to lead, to inspire and to teach". In terms of a vocational direction, many of the paths she was considering would have those opportunities. In some ways, the action of the vocation is secondary to life purpose. It didn't really matter if she went into city planning, city government or social work, all of those vocations would have presented opportunities for her "to lead, to inspire or to teach."

Another thing to consider is that our life purpose and our vocation may or may not crisscross. Some healers are fortunate enough to have their life purpose cross with their vocation. Other people have vocations that are purposeful for making money and then they do healing work as the spirit guides lead them to others.

You may have a vocation as an accountant but be the person that everyone comes to and confides in. People sense you will listen to them and they feel safe to communicate with you.

Many people work years in their vocation while developing their passion. It can take a long time to perfect a craft or have the maturity and discipline to manifest a life goal. I notice for some people there is a point in life where they finally let go of comfortable work and make sacrifices to live their purpose. Other people wait until retirement to jump into their artwork or start a pursuit that is more aligned with their creative or healing side.

For some people, they need to add "passion projects" to their life. Passion projects often fulfill your life purpose, but may have little to do with your vocation. A passion project is a type of work or hobby that you do in addition to working a job. You might do something charitable, or find a service project. You might run a half marathon for a good cause you believe in. You might make a craft and sell it online as a side income. Those are the types of projects that not only benefit you and others, but assist the world to be a better place.

And there are those of us who are determined to have our life vocation and life purpose be the same pursuit. Long hours and hard work pay off when your job doesn't feel like work because you enjoy your task and purpose in the work every day.

It's important to remember that raising a family or being the provider for a family is a life purpose. Many of us have to move through family life before we can change directions and do what we really want to do. Other people have high-powered system jobs that allow for them to travel or give generously to organizations they care about. In this way, the vocation is contributing to their life purpose even if they feel the vocation is not directly tied to the passion of their heart.

We are supposed to be excited about life and co-creating an abundant future. The guides are willing to help you co-create what you want to achieve. We have to search for our desires. This is why we must state our intentions and move in directions that assist us in manifesting what we want to create.

Life path questions in terms of life purpose, soul mate, career, business and family are important and you should ask them. But allow for time to pass and allow your life to unfold. The guides will only be able to tell you so much information, then it's more of a wait and see what develops in your life. If you ask the same life path questions over and over, it's hard to keep the conversation fresh and interesting. My suggestion is that you only ask the life path question once a month, or once in a while. See what answers you get, then be patient. Wait and see what happens as your life unfolds.

I use the example of allowing doors to open and close without you taking things personally. In the unfolding of your life, doors are opening and doors are closing. We watch for opportunities and new places to move towards. At the same time, if doors start to close, we notice a shift and time for change. Some events change your direction. Move with it. Be fluid and flexible. And if life is moving too slowly for you, or feels boring like no doors are opening, then shake things up, do something different. Don't be afraid to find a door and open it. Be open to what may come, as you check out what is on the other side of this door.

This section provides a list of life path questions that you can ask your guides. Keep in mind that these questions should be asked occasionally and not daily. If you ask the same questions over and over, the guides are likely to become quiet. Also these questions are very emotional. Sometimes our emotions prevent us from getting the correct answer. It may not be the answer that we want to hear or we may not be ready to make the move our guidance team hopes we would take.

Your life purpose is a big question. Often times it grows or changes its course. It's okay to not know your life purpose and continue to pursue education and interests, knowing that you will ultimately find yourself. Your guides will act as counselors. What is important is that you keep moving forward and don't get stuck or bored. Life is supposed to be an adventure, keep traveling. One thing is for certain, once you find your purpose, you are not bored and you feel fired up about what you are pursuing.

Life Purpose & Career Questions

Below are examples of life purpose questions. Notice that appropriate questions have these three features: the question shows you did your research, you use scaling questions, some actions have occurred and you are wondering how to react or respond.

Line of Questions for Career Searching
- Is it time for me to start a new career?
- Do I need a formal education to allow my vocation and life purpose to be the same?
- Looking at this list of types of jobs, what direction should I search?
- Using a scaling question, how risky is it to start a new business?
- If I keep my current job, will I have time for a side project?
- I want to make a change, but should I wait for a certain event to occur? (kids going to school)
- I got a job offer, but am not sure if I should take it. Should I try it out?
- I feel anxious when I go to work, should I start searching for something new?
- I didn't get the raise I wanted, should I continue to work for this company?
- Will my energy level and high frequency be a good fit for this organization?

Line of Questions for Life Purpose
- I want to do more meaningful work, what kind of healing work should I pursue? Make a list of types of healing work you are interested in and use scaling questions.
- I have always wanted to pursue my art or craft, is now a good time to start? Should I count on my art or craft as my source of income? How long might it take me to get established?
- I am not happy with my current job, should I do something more creative? Should I do my creative work on the side, or take a risk and change to a more creative career?
- Is my life purpose and my vocation supposed to be the same? Can I express my life purpose in my current job setting?
- When I think about my life purpose, I imagine it has to do with these activities. Can you scale this list for me? Teaching, Leading Groups, Writing Books, Counseling, Energy Healing.
- Has my current job served its purpose? I am not as fulfilled as I used to be. I only have five more years until I retire or meet another financial goal, should I wait it out?
- What is holding me back from making a change? List items on your fingers. Are these points valid? Is fear holding me back from moving forward?
- If I pay for this certification, will it lead me in the direction of my life purpose?

Less Appropriate Line of Questions
Less appropriate questions may not provide enough information for you to make a good decision. These questions are simple yes/no and don't leave room for a conversation. They may have a fear-based component or ask a forecasting question that is inappropriate.

- Can I quit my job? I can't stand my manager.
- If I apply for this job will I get it?
- When will I run out of money?
- Should I take a job even though I don't want it?

Relationship Questions

Our human nature drives us towards relationships. Most people want to be in intimate relationships, but it's challenging to find the right partner. Most people want to have strong family relationships, but often family members can feel toxic or unsafe for you. Roommates can be difficult to live with. Relationships with friends can come and go, or we move to a different location and have to build new relationships.

The primary way I ask about relationships is by using this simple question. "Has the relationship served its purpose?" This question is more appropriate than, "Should I break up this person?" or "Should I ask my roommate to move out?" or "Should I unfriend this person from social media?"

We attract relationships to teach us about ourselves. Anyone we share our life with holds up a mirror for us to self-evaluate and grow. This section focuses on how best to use the pendulum to ask questions about intimate relationships.

If you are a single person and looking for a partner, I understand that the primary question is, "Is this person my soul mate or twin flame?" My definition of soul mate is any intimate relationship that comes in to teach you about yourself. This relationship can be long term or short term. A twin flame is someone that you share a deep soulful connection with and usually both of you share the same purpose. A twin flame may be a marriage relationship, but it can also be a life partner that helps you establish a common goal. A twin flame can also be on the other side in the astral world and assisting you from afar.

In our modern world, intimate relationships may or may not last a lifetime. The length of time depends on a number of factors, like personality differences, vices, lifestyle differences, family influences, work-related issues and dependency issues, to name a few. The most important thing for the lightworker to understand is that when a person moves in the direction of ascension, sometimes they spiritually outgrow their partners.

When someone shows up in my office and wants the answer to the question, "Is this person my soul mate?" I normally say the guides are unwilling to answer that question for at least three months. Come back after some time has passed and we can revisit. In the present moment, with this new love interest, have fun, and be nonattached.

I will answer questions such as, "How many lifetimes have I spent with this person? What was the nature of the relationship, positive or negative? Is this a karmic relationship or a new relationship?" A karmic relationship means there is unfinished business that needs to be resolved. Karmic relationships are often more rocky and meant for growth, rather than support and a peaceful time.

One of the reasons the guides will not answer the question "is this person my soul mate", is because if there is chemistry and motivation to get to know this person, then why would the guides give you a message to walk away? Chemistry and physical attraction is a signal that there is a reason to get to know this person. There is something this person is going to teach you; even if the person is teaching you about unhealthy patterns and areas to improve in your life. There is something you have to gain. Will the relationship be long standing or life long, well, the answer is, "wait and see" or "come back and ask after the chemistry fades a bit and we can look at how the relationship is evolving."

Normally after the first three months and definitely after the next six months, the soul mate question is naturally answered based on how events unfold. As chemistry naturally subsides and the couple moves into a long standing relationship, the honeymoon period wears off and you can see the positives and negatives of sharing time with this person. Every relationship has patterns, you can either tolerate the pattern or you decide to move on.

Everyone should enjoy chemistry, and then, as the relationship settles, can ask, "Is this relationship worth pursuing long term? Is this person my soul mate? Would they make a good life partner?" Another issue with chemistry is, emotions are heightened. It can be hard to read the pendulum when your emotions really want the relationship to be long term. Your emotions can override a clear communication with your guides or clear thinking. It just takes time to learn moods, behaviors, and positive and negative coping skills of a person.

Breaking up is the hardest thing to do. There is nothing worse than breaking up after a long-term relationship. It's hard on many levels: disintegration of family, losing your home life, untangling finances and co-parenting. Starting over takes patience and the willingness to be alone. There is dating and getting back out there.

Often times people will come in and ask if their guides feel they should break up. I use the question, "Has the relationship served its purpose?" Because once the relationship has served its purpose, it's time to move on. There may be other issues that keep the relationship necessary, like finances or need to formulate an exit plan.

Many times the answer is "Yes, the relationship has served its purpose." Even when clients hear this, they don't normally run home and ask for a divorce. There is a struggle and it takes a long time before they are ready to make a change. They may feel guilty about hurting the other person. They may not want to lose family members, or are afraid of being judged by others. It may take time to realize you are personally tired of feeling hurt by the other person. You may need to give time to the situation to see if the person will be capable of or is willing to make changes.

Relationships are complex and emotional. If you find yourself stuck and not able to move forward, seek a life coach or counselor to assist in you in finding resolution to maintaining or ending relationships. Have patience, see how you feel and allow for movement and change when it's called for.

Below are suggested questions to start a conversation with your guides. These questions pertain to intimate relationships, but can also apply to roommates, friends and family members. Use the line of questions below to start a conversation with your guides. Remember, ask Life Path questions occasionally and not daily.

Line of Questions for Intimate Relationships

- Has this relationship served its purpose? Is it time to taper the relationship or break away?

- Is this relationship in my highest best interest?

- This person has some behaviors that bother me, do I work with them, or do I walk away?

- I can identify an unhealthy pattern in our relationship. Is this pattern likely to repeat?

- I really like my new partner, but they have a difficult family, can I work with that, or should I walk away?

- My heart feels like something is off, can I trust my instincts? Should I approach them?

- Does this person have positive coping skills for life challenges?

- Does this person know how to relax?

- Reviewing this behavior, is this a negative vice that I should consider a red flag?

- I notice an unhealthy pattern forming in the relationship. Is it likely to improve or are we no longer aligned?

- I really want a commitment with this person, but it feels like they are less likely to want to get serious. Should I stay and wait for a commitment or should I take it as a signal that it's time to make a change?.

Less Appropriate Line of Questions

Less appropriate questions around relationships tend to be gossipy or asking the guides to tell you about cheating. The other questions are fear based or show your insecurities. Remember to trust your instincts and feelings in your heart. Hold off on asking if the person is a soul mate until your relationship has developed and you have gotten to know their character. Often times, their behaviors in the first few months will answer that question for you.

- Is this new person I met my soul mate? [Wait 3-6 months before you ask this.]

- How many partners has this person had?

- Is this person seeing someone else?

- Can I trust this person, are they cheating on me?

- Should I call the person or wait to see if they call me?

- Will this person make a good father?

- Is this person using me?

- Does this person like someone else more than me?

Metaphysical Questions

While our angelic teams don't mind answering our most pressing questions about life purpose, career and relationships, the guides prefer to focus on our health, healing and metaphysical questions. Life path questions should be asked occasionally, but metaphysical questions can be asked often or daily. The guides find this line of questioning more interesting and productive for growth and ascension. As we heal ourselves, we eventually begin to heal other people.

I developed a strong relationship with my guides because I had an endless fascination with metaphysics. I had questions about meditation, dimensions, spiritual hierarchies, hypnosis, past lives, crystals and the astral realms.

I had questions about the universe, starseeds and galactics. I had questions about dreamtime and dream interpretations. I would read a book on a subject and then stop to ask my guides questions about what I was reading. Did my guides agree or disagree? How might they scale the author's interpretation?

I felt like I was a metaphysical journalist that gained access to angels in the astral plane and could ask any questions that came to mind. My curiosity kept me up late into the evening hours interested and communicating interactively.

At first I used the pendulum to learn about my angelic team. Then I explored energy healing and chakra balancing. As time moved on I used the pendulum to ask questions about "What herbs should I be taking?" "How many Echinacea should I take today?" "Do I really need to seek medical treatment for this issue?" "What is the health of my organs?" "How many days a week should I work out?" "Was I getting enough protein?" "Do crystals have consciousness?" "What type of essential oil blends should I create?" "How many oils should I use?" On and on, I always found a reason to ask a question and I was fascinated at the conversations that would follow.

In this section I present metaphysical questions. These are sample questions to get you thinking about what you might ask, or how you might want to expand the conversation.

Your angelic team encourages you to explore secret knowledge and inspire your life. Use these sample questions to assist you in getting started having a metaphysical conversation with your angelic team.

Questions and conversations related to the chakras and energy healing can be found in the next book in this series called "Chakra Balancing with the Pendulum".

Meditation

- How many ways does meditation benefit me? Examine the 5 Aspects of Yourself: Physical, Mental, Emotional, Energetic and Spiritual.

- How long should I meditate today? Should I move into expanded meditation space, or should I focus on working with my guides?

- Is there anything the guides would like to show me? How many things? Let's begin, relax and wait for an image to come to you. Go with your first instinct. What comes to your mind?

Mediumship

- Are there any attachments on me? If "Yes", how many? Where did they come from? Can you assist me in crossing them over and releasing them from my auric field? How long will it take?

- I saw an angel sign. A feather was on the ground. I wonder if it came from my grandmother (who is crossed-over). I keep thinking about her. Was it her? Does she have a message for me? Meditate and tune into the energy. You can sit in the quiet or allow a vision to come to you. At the conclusion of your meditation, release the experience into the light.

Angel Signs

- I keep seeing 444. What do the synchronicities mean? Think about what you were thinking about when you saw the numbers.

- There are many interpretations of 444 online. Make a list, assign items to your fingers. "Does the number have to do with numerology?" "Do you want me to take an action?" "Are you just letting me know that you're present with me today?" "Do the number signs mean I am advancing on my path of ascension?"

Astrology

- Ask general questions about the practice of astrology.

- Which of these transits should I pay attention to? What is this transit trying to teach me? How many items? You receive the answer "3". Allow the answers to come to your mind and write them down.

- What is the best interpretation for this transit? Give the guides options. Assign items to fingers. Narrow or hone the best answer this way.

Numerology

- I keep seeing the sign 777 and 333. What do the numbers mean to me? Why am I receiving this angel sign? Are these numbers personal to me, or should I reference the numerology meaning? Ask other questions about number patterns you become aware of.

- Ask general questions about the practice of numerology. If you ask questions about your interpretation, you can validate or get more information by consulting your guides.

Dream Interpretation

- I had a dream last night. I remember a cat I used to have was in the dream. I remember writing in my journal in a small house. It felt like there were no doors. What is the meaning of this dream? Does this dream represent a subconscious fear or something else?

- Keep a dream journal. When you notice a repeating symbol, ask questions to the guides about the meaning of the symbol. I saw a "pile of small rocks" in the back of my "old childhood house". How many things does the "pile of small rocks" represent?

- How important was the dream I had last night? Did something significant occur? Was I dreaming or was I astral traveling?

Astral Travel in Dreamtime

- Did I astral travel in dreamtime? I feel like I went somewhere. Did I go to meet with my guides? How many were there? What did we speak about, how many items? See what comes to you.

- Did I go to meet other entities last night? Did I meet with galactic beings? How much time passed last night relative to this time stream?

The purpose of this work is to assist you in developing a relationship with your angelic team and assist you in developing your psychic skills. The more you communicate with the pendulum, the more a telepathy link is formed. As you focus on your health and healing, the faster you will reach optimal health. As you heal yourself, you become ready to heal other people. Your own research and process of asking questions teaches you about the topics you are investigating. This is the goal of everyone's angelic team, to assist their candidate in healing and ascension and to help them to heal others.

Asking "How" or "Why" Questions

Divination tools are pointers along your path. While the pendulum can give you a lot of information, questioning with the instrument is not designed to give you "how" and "why" answers. However, as your relationship and communication skills develop, you can start to receive "how" and "why" answers through developing your clairsentient and clairaudient skills.

Another way to phrase a "how" or "why" question is with the number question. For example, "How many reasons is this happening to me?" You may receive the answer "3". Next sit quietly with this answer. Ask your guides if they will give you the 3 reasons psychically. Meditate and clear your mind. Await a message or knowingness of the answer. A message will come to you. You may receive the answer, "It is time to move on. You know you are not happy here." Or you may already have a good idea of why something is occurring. Ask your guides, "Is this happening because of this reason? You can then receive a "Yes" or "No" or another answer. Make an assumption and then ask for a validation with the pendulum.

If you know the first and second answer, but can't figure out the third reason, again, meditate for a minute and see what comes to you. On a few occasions I remember feeling like, I just don't know what you are trying to communicate with me. I might ask, "Will you give me a letter?" I might receive a letter visually, or use the alphabet chart. I would then meditate again to see if that letter made me aware of the answer.

In the beginning of my practice, I might even channel in the entire word with the alphabet chart. If you do this, ask for how many letters are in the word, and then start to channel it in. You may get a word like "pattern". If a word comes in and it is not clear to you, sit and meditate and you will receive more information. The thought might come to you, "Okay, I am repeating the same pattern." The question comes, "Why is this pattern repeating itself, what I am trying to gain from this experience?" Rephrase the question, "How many things do I need to do to stop repeating this pattern?" Ask for a number and keep awaiting the response until you receive the answers you seek.

As you grow, trusting your intuition becomes easier. If you get a letter, almost always, the rest of the word or answer will come. If you get a word, the phrase or meaning of the word will make sense to you. If you keep on with this practice, eventually the communication will grow, you will know deeply that you are very intuitive and in communication with your guides.

Chapter 10. Health, Healing Questions & Charts

The angelic guides enjoy answering questions that are focused on health and healing. Like metaphysical questions these types of questions benefit our growth and move us in the direction of optimal healing. It wasn't until after my psychic opening that I started asking about herbal products. I became aware that I could ask questions about herbs I was considering taking. Was the herb beneficial to me and how much should I use? The guides love to answer questions about herbal supplements and vitamins. The guides prefer we use natural medicine for preventative care and bolstering our immunity and organs.

When I first started asking about health and healing, I would use the pendulum in two ways. I would pendulum on the hand, or would pull out the products and hold the pendulum over them to see if I got a "Yes" or "No" answer. If I got a "Yes" I would then ask, "How much of this product should I take and how many times a day?" I always wanted to know which angel or guide was speaking to me.

I started to pendulum over my essential oils and crystals. If I had a question about which crystal would benefit me, I would hold the pendulum over the crystal and await the answer "Yes" or "No". I would ask which essential oils to wear. I would hold the pendulum over the group of oils. I might ask the guides, which column and which row. I found I could use the pendulum like a tool to find the correct answer out of the group of items.

There were other times when I needed to use larger lists of information to draw out the answers. I found that for some questions, it was better to create charts. Charts were helpful for holding lists of information. Plus, I could write on the charts and make meaningful marks that assisted me with communication. I enjoyed producing charts and got very creative.

In this chapter, I move through three topics that you can explore with your guides to improve your health and healing practices. The three sections are: vitamin and herbs, nutrition and exercise, crystals and essential oils.

In many cases you may want to customize your own charts. The charts provided in this chapter are useful, but you may want to add different information. Included in the material are two blank charts for you to create your own charts. One chart is the half circle and the other is almost a full circle. I encourage you to make photocopies and create your own charts.

Included is an example of a creative chart called "Do Something Positive". You can use the charts to find positive activities your guides suggest you do. These activities will raise your frequency. See how the pendulum swings for you. As you move through the material, think about the chart you feel inspired to create.

Vitamins and Herbs

Make sure to clear the energy body and ask the validation questions. After you meditate for a few minutes, start working with your guides to find out about what supplements can strengthen your body and make you feel optimal. Ask your healing guides to come in and make suggestions about what kinds of vitamins and herbs you should take.

There are several techniques to use the pendulum with vitamins and herbs. The first way is to dangle the pendulum over the herbal product and see if the swing of the pendulum signals "Yes" or "No". A "Yes" answer would indicate that the herbal product is beneficial for you. You could then ask a scaling question, "On a scale from 1 to 6, how beneficial is this product? 5 or 6 would be beneficial and you should continue to take these supplements. A 3 or 4 score would indicate that your body is neutral and you could take it or leave it. A 1 or 2 score would mean it's not worth the cost of the product, your body doesn't really need it.

The third way to ask a question is by using a pendulum chart. The vitamin and herb chart provided in this chapter has a list of well known vitamins and herbs. Use the chart to ask if there is any supplement you should research or consider taking. Charts can be very handy for working with clients. When using a pendulum chart, first ask, "How many types of supplements on this chart would be helpful for my body?"

You may get the answer "2". Great, now you understand you are looking to receive two answers. Channel in the two answers by allowing the pendulum to dangle and move to the correct entries. For this introduction chart, you don't have to know exactly what the supplements do, you can still receive an answer from the guides. If you get an answer like "Vitamin D", do a quick internet search and find out how Vitamin D can assist your body. This chart is a short list to assist you in getting started.

You can make a personalized pendulum chart and customize it with your own vitamins and herbs. You can start with a list that is from your pantry. You can also find a list of herbal supplements on the internet and use that as a way to create your chart. You can use the number chart or pendulum on the hand to find out information about dosing vitamins and herbs daily. Ask "How many capsules should I take each day?"

You can also use a list from your favorite catalog of products. As you read over the list, ask your guides to give you a clockwise motion over the supplements that should be put on your personal chart. If you are creating a chart from scratch with a blank chart, you would want to research the items you are placing on the chart. The research doesn't have to be intensive, just that you know a little bit about each product. You would also understand the purpose of your chart and what information you are trying to gather.

You can also pendulum on the hand and have a conversation about vitamins and herbs. Consider these questions to get the conversation started.

Questions to Ask About Vitamins and Herbs

Below are questions to ask to start a conversation about Vitamins and Herbs. Other helpful ideas are given to help you create a personal list for yourself. Remember to clear and meditate. Remember to use the validation questions.

- Are there any vitamins and herbs that you think would be helpful for my body? How many items on the chart will you show me? If you get the number 5, watch for the pendulum to swing to five items on the chart.

- Please scale these health and healing products. What is the most beneficial for me?

- On a scale from 1 to 6, can you let me know which products are essential for my body? Your guides are encouraging you to continue taking whatever items are ranked at 5 or 6.

- What herbs should I be taking? How many caplets?

- Should I take the supplement daily or weekly?

- How many times a days should I take this supplement?

- How many times a week should I take this supplement?

- How is the vitamin or supplement assisting my body? Do a search on the internet and find out common ways this vitamin or supplement supports the body. For example, Vitamin A is useful for immunity, vision, reproduction, cellular growth and maintaining organs. Assign items to fingers. Find out why your guides are recommending it for your body.

- I feel like I am coming down with a cold, what should I take, what remedy should I try?

- How many Echinacea [or name of another herb] should I take if I want to boost my immunity?

- Should I purchase Echinacea and Goldenseal together or apart? It is sold both ways.

- I read in an article that Echinacea will boost your immunity, do I have to take it every day? Or just when I am sick?

VITAMINS AND HERBS

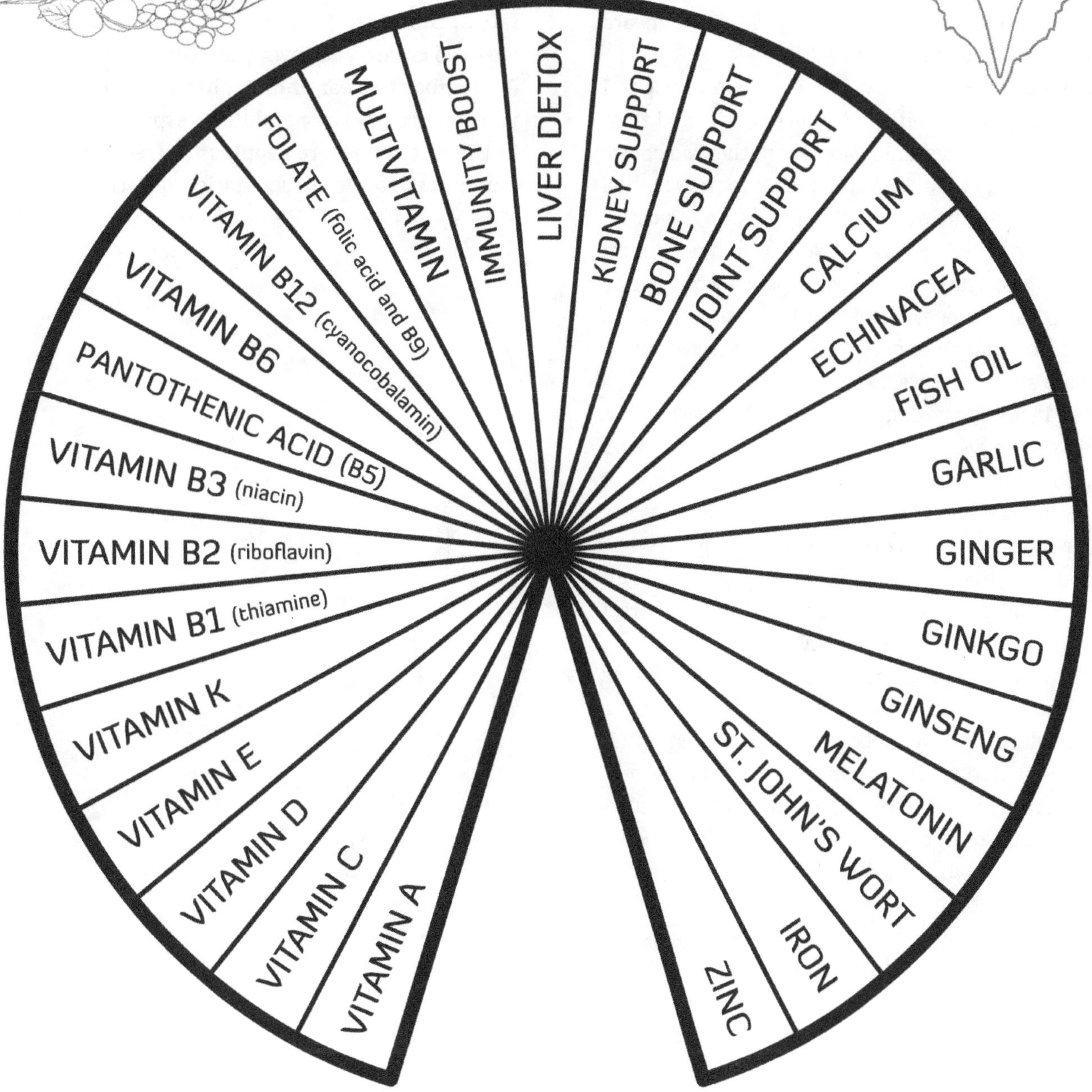

- FOLATE (folic acid and B9)
- MULTIVITAMIN
- IMMUNITY BOOST
- LIVER DETOX
- KIDNEY SUPPORT
- BONE SUPPORT
- JOINT SUPPORT
- CALCIUM
- ECHINACEA
- FISH OIL
- GARLIC
- GINGER
- GINKGO
- GINSENG
- MELATONIN
- ST. JOHN'S WORT
- IRON
- ZINC
- VITAMIN A
- VITAMIN C
- VITAMIN D
- VITAMIN E
- VITAMIN K
- VITAMIN B1 (thiamine)
- VITAMIN B2 (riboflavin)
- VITAMIN B3 (niacin)
- PANTOTHENIC ACID (B5)
- VITAMIN B6
- VITAMIN B12 (cyanocobalamin)

Raven shamballa©
www.ravenlightbody.com

Nutrition and Exercise

Everyone wants to improve their health through diet and exercise. Your guides are more than happy to assist you with nutritional questions you might have. An angel or guide specializing in healthy eating will come forward to assist you in meeting your goals.

I remember one January, I wanted to lose weight. I made an agreement with my guides that I would not eat anything that they didn't approve. If the food choice was okay to eat, I got a "Yes" and if not, I got a "No" and I didn't eat it. I went through my refrigerator and threw out everything that received a "No". I would pendulum over fruits and vegetables. I was surprised when I got a "No" for potatoes, for example, but I eliminated it from my diet. For that time period my guides asked me to eliminate all dairy as well.

Then I took the next step of asking, "Is this the right portion size for weight loss?" I was surprised. My angels let me know my portion sizes were too big. I remember I could eat vegetable marinara sauce but kept getting a "No" for the spaghetti. When I cut the spaghetti to less than half, the pendulum swung to "Yes". This was instant feedback. I used the pendulum to assist me in correct portion size and by March, I lost twenty pounds.

I started to ask questions about gluten-free products and other protein drinks. I wanted feedback on nutritional products that would be helpful for me or neutral for me. I wanted to understand, "What was the best solution for my body?" I would pendulum over products for "Yes" and "No", and I regularly scaled a new product idea for my body. If the product didn't get a 5 or 6 on my scale, I didn't purchase it.

One time a client came in with food sensitivities and asked me this question, "My colitis is acting up, are there foods my guides feel I should not eat?" I put together a fruit and vegetable chart to assist people in these types of questions.

In the charts at the end of the section, I present a fruit and vegetable chart to assist you in practicing to ask questions.

Below are suggested questions based on the fruit and vegetable chart. You can apply these questions to other types of food, like proteins, fats or processed food you eat. Use the blank chart to create your own nutrition charts. Remember to clear and meditate before you start to use the pendulum, especially in the kitchen where people may frequent. Remember to use the validation questions.

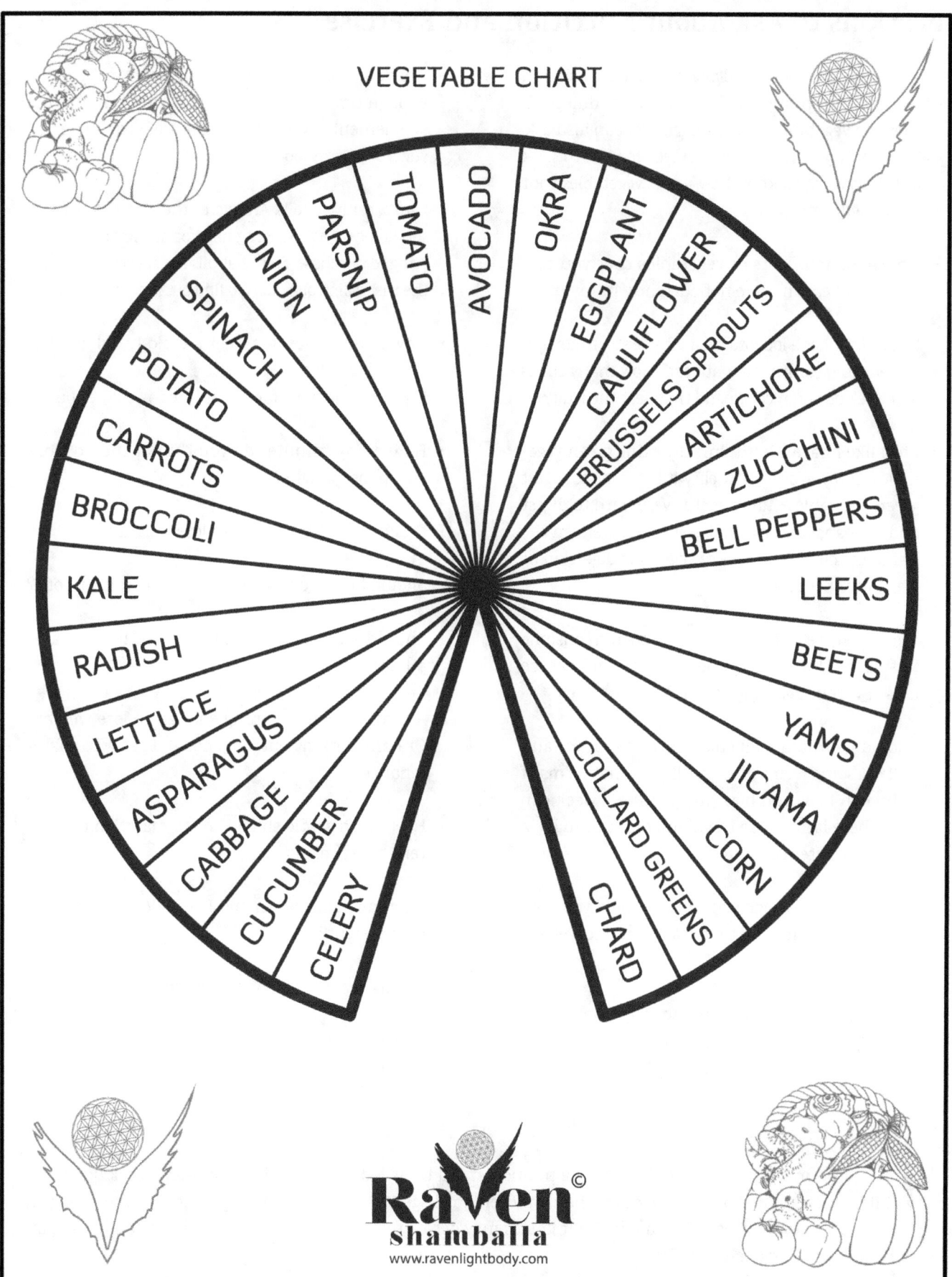

Questions to Ask About Nutrition and Exercise

- Are there any fruits and vegetables that I should eliminate from my diet? Allow the pendulum to move to vegetables in the chart. You can also ask, "How many items will you select for me to look at?" This way you know how many vegetables your guides will comment on.

- Are there any fruits or vegetables that you recommend I eat that are not currently in my diet?

- I know fruit has a lot of sugar, are there still fruits that you would recommend that I eat? How many times in a week do you recommend that I eat the fruit?

- I feel like I have a hard time digesting green vegetables. Can you scale how easy it is for me to digest green vegetables? 1 means it is very hard to digest and 6 means it is easy to digest. Use fingers on the hand for scaling the ease of vegetable digestion or use a number chart.

- I really like ice cream, but I know I should consume less dairy. How many times a week can I eat ice cream without gaining weight?

- Should I eliminate all dairy from my diet? Can I still eat some forms of dairy? If yes, what forms of dairy can I eat and how many times a week can I eat these items? Use the blank chart to make a list of dairy items.

- Am I drinking enough water? How would you scale my daily water intake? On a scale from 1 to 6 where is my hydration for today?

- What are the best proteins for my body? How many times a week should I eat proteins?

- I have a vegetarian or vegan diet. Am I getting enough protein in my diet? Should I take protein supplements? What other kinds of protein do you suggest for my body?

- I am sensitive to oils. Are there other types of oil that I should be using? Make a chart for oils you are considering to purchase. See what oils are suggested for you. Use the scaling questions to find out more information.

- How many times in a week should I work out?

- If I work out hard for 20 minutes, is that enough?

- How many minutes do you think I should work out to lose weight?

- Do I need to lift weights to lose weight?

- Should I focus on weight training, cardio or both?

- Should I focus on a mat exercise like yoga or pilates?

- Are my workouts strong enough to lose weight? Or I am working out just enough to stay in maintenance?

- How much cardio should I do to maintain my current body weight?

- How much cardio should I do to lose my current body weight?

- Is walking enough to help me to lose weight?

- How much time would I have to walk daily to lose weight?

I have a question about my child. I am trying to understand their food sensitivities. Is it okay to ask questions for my child? (Parents hold psychic space for their children until age 10, 12 or 14, depending on the independency of the child.) Make sure to ask permission first. Your guides may decide to consult with a guide from your child's team before you begin asking questions.

FRUIT CHART

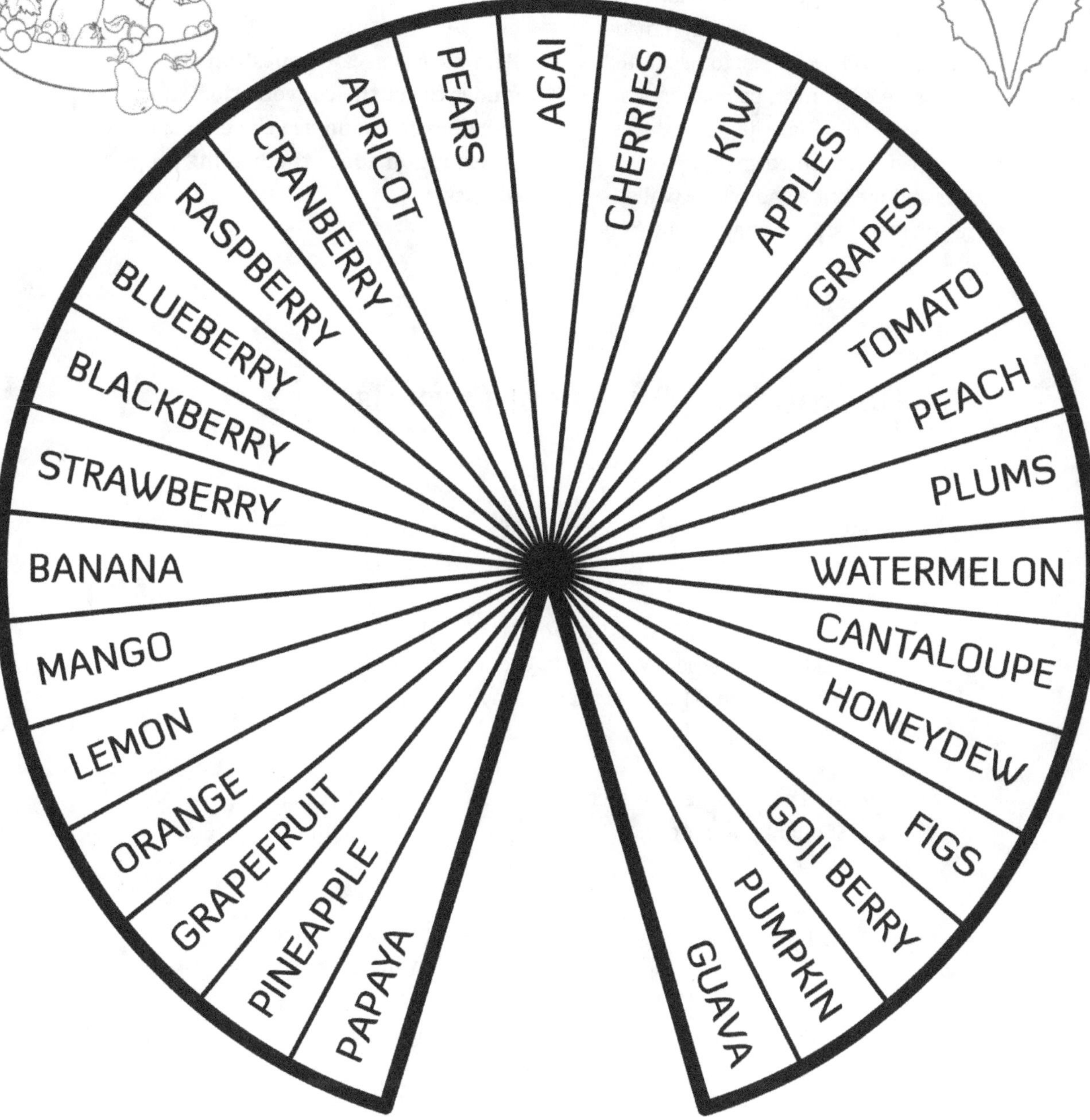

- APRICOT
- PEARS
- ACAI
- CHERRIES
- KIWI
- APPLES
- GRAPES
- TOMATO
- PEACH
- PLUMS
- WATERMELON
- CANTALOUPE
- HONEYDEW
- FIGS
- GOJI BERRY
- PUMPKIN
- GUAVA
- PAPAYA
- PINEAPPLE
- GRAPEFRUIT
- ORANGE
- LEMON
- MANGO
- BANANA
- STRAWBERRY
- BLACKBERRY
- BLUEBERRY
- RASPBERRY
- CRANBERRY

Raven© shamballa
www.ravenlightbody.com

Crystal & Essential Oil

As I progressed along my studies, I started to become interested in crystals and essential oils. Both of these items are magical and have healing properties that open your chakras, uplift your mood or enrich your day. I made a crystal chart and essential oil chart for you to get started with. I picked what I felt were the most popular crystals and essential oils people work with. Have fun asking questions and making your own customized charts.

Remember to clear and meditate and ask the validation question before you start using the pendulum. You can pendulum over the items and await "Yes" or "No" answers. Have fun asking the questions below.

Below are suggested questions to ask your guides to get the conversation started. Ask questions and use the charts to find out information about the healing properties of both.

Questions to Ask About Crystals

- What type of crystal should I buy to assist me in manifesting my goals? How many types of crystals do you suggest I use?

- I want to make a crystal grid for the purpose of improving my meditation. What type of grid should I make? What type of crystals should I use? Is there a way you want me to set the crystals up?

- Are there enough protection crystals in my home or office? Should I purchase more? What type of crystals should I purchase?

- Do I need to clear my crystals? Hold the pendulum over the crystal and see if you get a "Yes" or a "No" swing.

- What are the best crystals to clear my heart chakra?

- Is there a crystal that I can use to assist me in my creativity?

- This crystal has many purposes, in what way is the crystal assisting me? Assign the list to fingers, or make a chart.

- Do crystals have consciousness? Is there an angel, spirit guide, lost soul or another type of energy residing in this crystal?"

CRYSTAL CHART

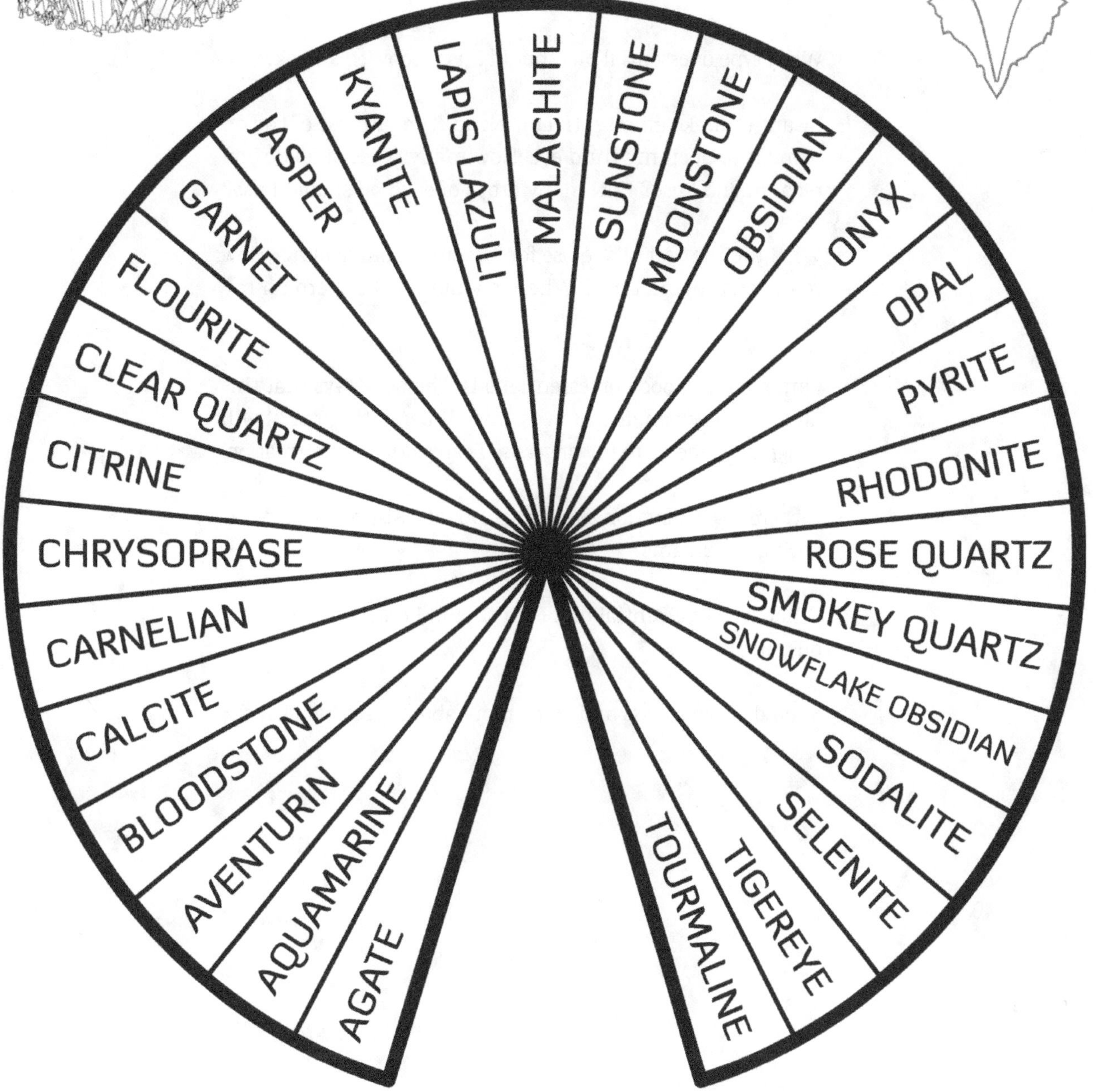

- JASPER
- KYANITE
- LAPIS LAZULI
- MALACHITE
- SUNSTONE
- MOONSTONE
- OBSIDIAN
- ONYX
- OPAL
- PYRITE
- RHODONITE
- ROSE QUARTZ
- SMOKEY QUARTZ
- SNOWFLAKE OBSIDIAN
- SODALITE
- SELENITE
- TIGEREYE
- TOURMALINE
- AGATE
- AQUAMARINE
- AVENTURIN
- BLOODSTONE
- CALCITE
- CARNELIAN
- CHRYSOPRASE
- CITRINE
- CLEAR QUARTZ
- FLOURITE
- GARNET

Raven shamballa
www.ravenlightbody.com

Questions to Ask About Essential Oils

- What type of essential oils should I use today/this week?

- I want to make an essential oil blend. The purpose of the oil blend is to open my third eye. How many types of oil do you recommend I use? How many drops of each oil should I use?

- What are the best oils to use for my emotional healing? How many oils should I use? Where should I place them on my body?

- I am reading a book on essential oils. The book says that this oil has many benefits. How is this oil benefiting me? I will assign the benefits to my fingers so I can get more information.

- Is there a combination of oils that would assist me in remembering my dreams?

- What type of essential oil blend should I create? How many oils should I use?

- Should I take a class and learn more about essential oils?

ESSENTIAL OILS

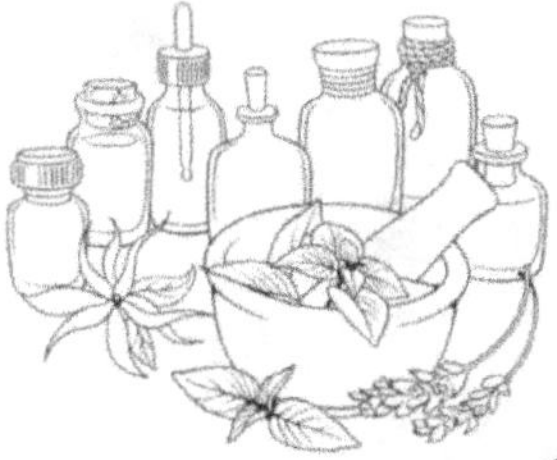

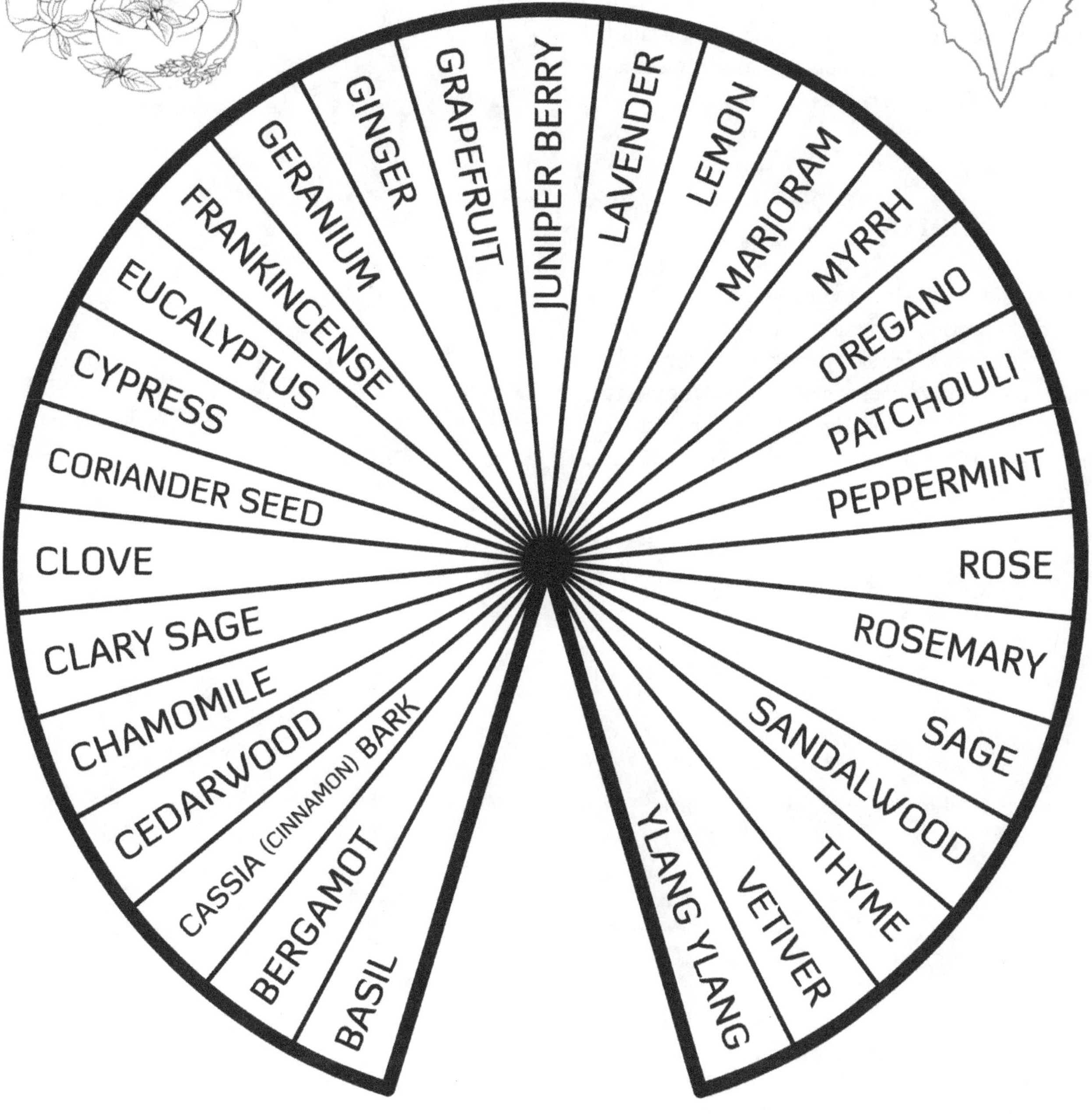

- GRAPEFRUIT
- GINGER
- GERANIUM
- FRANKINCENSE
- EUCALYPTUS
- CYPRESS
- CORIANDER SEED
- CLOVE
- CLARY SAGE
- CHAMOMILE
- CEDARWOOD
- CASSIA (CINNAMON) BARK
- BERGAMOT
- BASIL
- JUNIPER BERRY
- LAVENDER
- LEMON
- MARJORAM
- MYRRH
- OREGANO
- PATCHOULI
- PEPPERMINT
- ROSE
- ROSEMARY
- SAGE
- SANDALWOOD
- THYME
- VETIVER
- YLANG YLANG

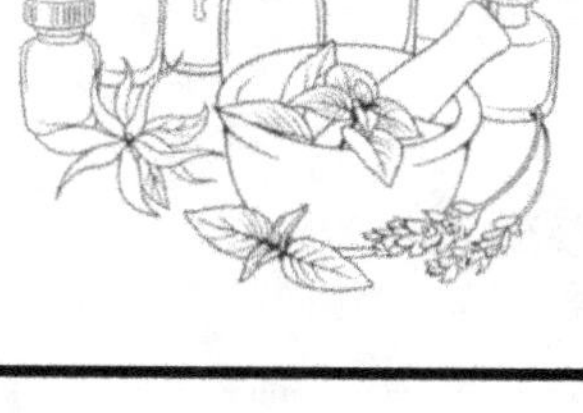

www.ravenlightbody.com

Blank Charts

This section also contains two blank charts. One is a half circle and the other is a full circle. Photocopy these charts and start to create your own charts, write in your own ideas that you are curious about asking. The chart that you decide to use depends on how much information you have to fill in the chart.

Creative Charts

Think outside of the box and make creative charts. The last chart I provide is an example of a creative chart. It is called "Shifting Your Mood to a Positive Vibration". This chart has positive coping skills you might use to raise your vibration to a positive place. You can come home and ask, "What activity should I do to shift my mood to a higher positive vibration?"

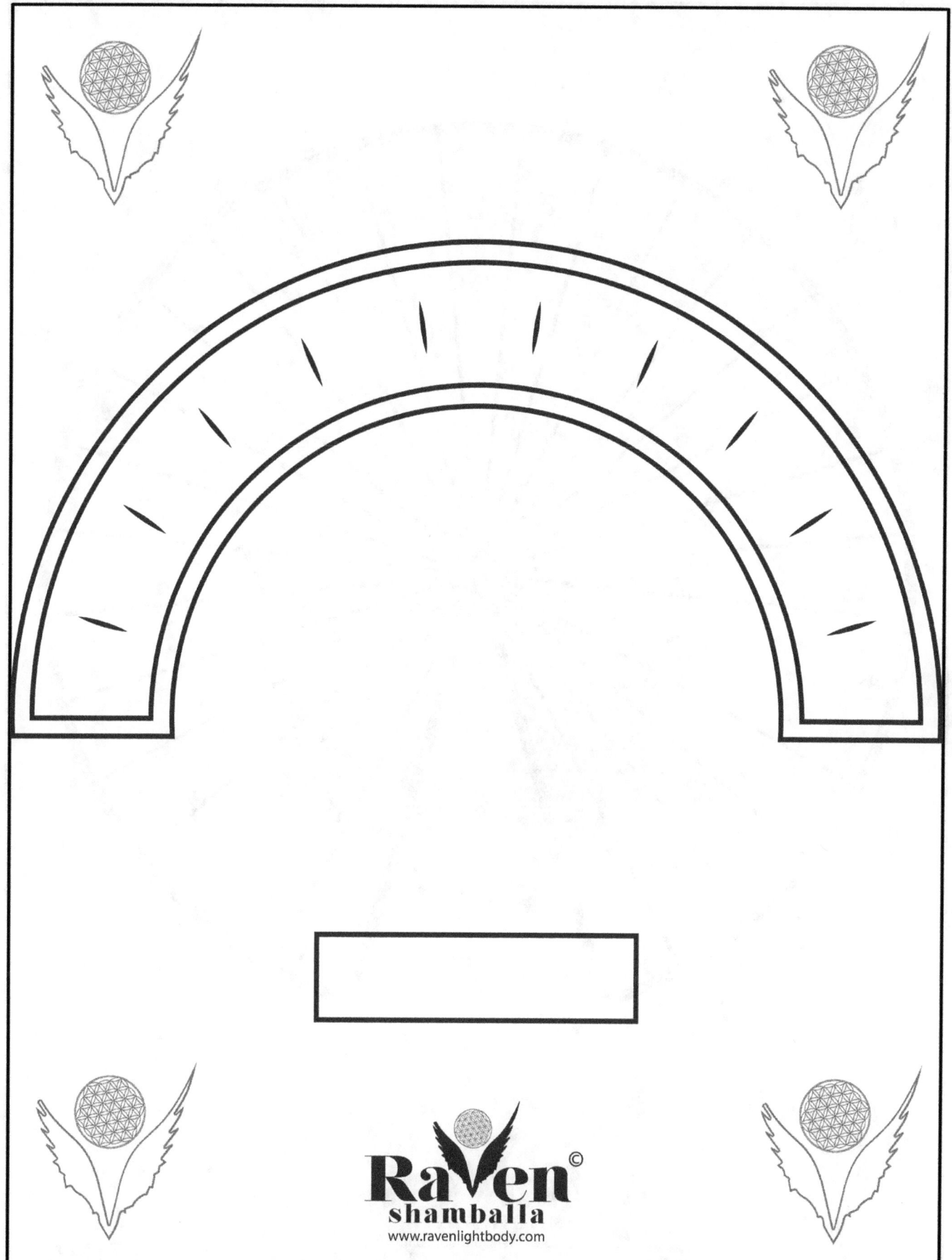

DO SOMETHING POSITIVE

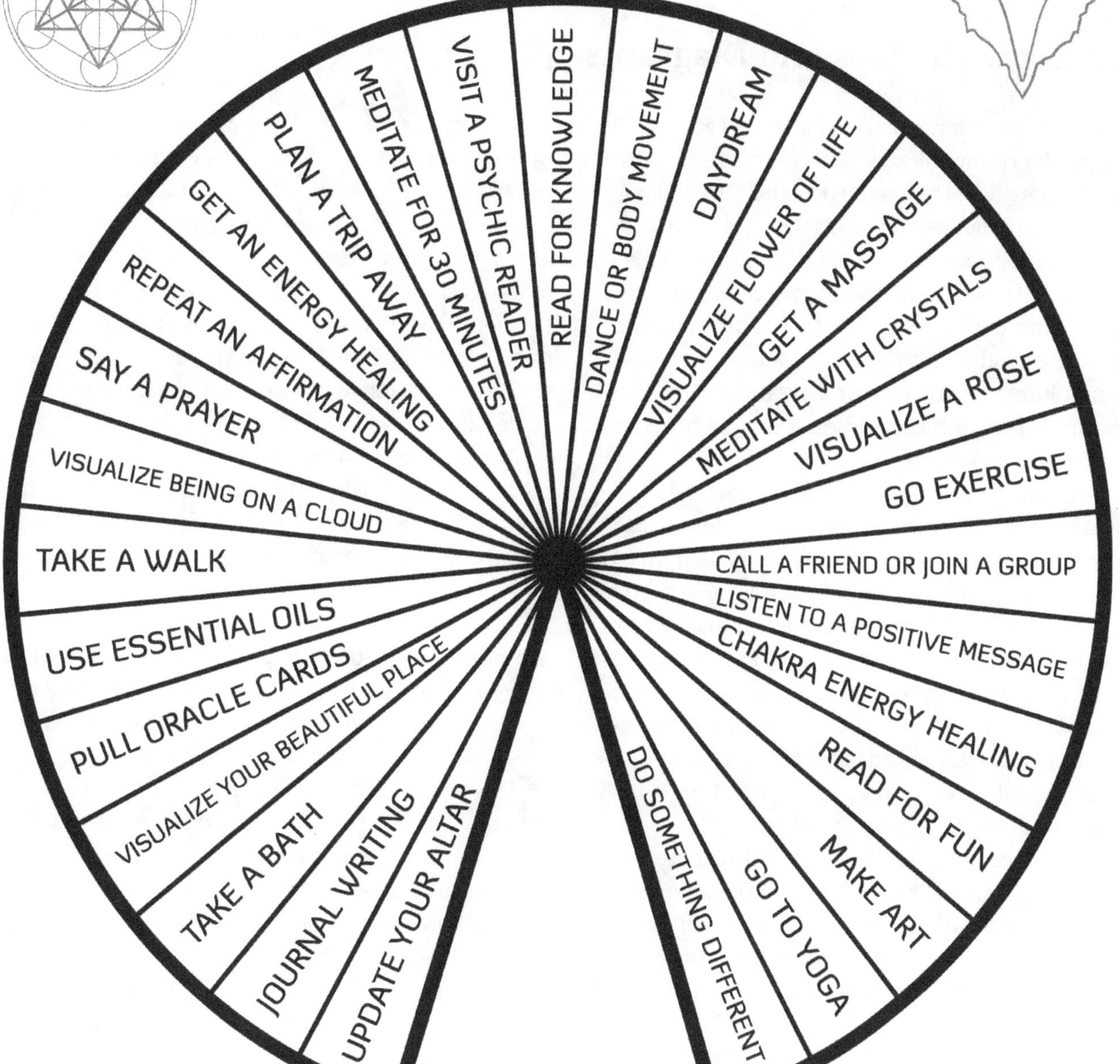

A wheel divided into segments, each labeled with a positive activity:

- VISIT A PSYCHIC READER
- MEDITATE FOR 30 MINUTES
- PLAN A TRIP AWAY
- GET AN ENERGY HEALING
- REPEAT AN AFFIRMATION
- SAY A PRAYER
- VISUALIZE BEING ON A CLOUD
- TAKE A WALK
- USE ESSENTIAL OILS
- PULL ORACLE CARDS
- VISUALIZE YOUR BEAUTIFUL PLACE
- TAKE A BATH
- JOURNAL WRITING
- UPDATE YOUR ALTAR
- READ FOR KNOWLEDGE
- DANCE OR BODY MOVEMENT
- DAYDREAM
- VISUALIZE FLOWER OF LIFE
- GET A MASSAGE
- MEDITATE WITH CRYSTALS
- VISUALIZE A ROSE
- GO EXERCISE
- CALL A FRIEND OR JOIN A GROUP
- LISTEN TO A POSITIVE MESSAGE
- CHAKRA ENERGY HEALING
- READ FOR FUN
- MAKE ART
- GO TO YOGA
- DO SOMETHING DIFFERENT

www.ravenlightbody.com

Chapter 11. Maps & Diagrams

Working with Maps and Diagrams

This course in pendulum work has given you several techniques for communication with your angelic team. There are many ways to use the pendulum to find out information. This last section covers the topic of working with maps and diagrams. Working with maps and diagrams has a slightly different technique called "casting" the pendulum onto a surface. Rather than using the swing of the pendulum to reveal the answer, you cast the pendulum onto the map or diagram. Casting the pendulum is the word that closest describes how the pendulum responds.

You cast the pendulum downward towards the map, there is a subtle weight that pulls the pendulum to the exact location. You are not throwing the pendulum or even intending the pendulum to land, it is more subtle than that. The pendulum will feel pulled to an exact point and put itself down on the map. This is similar to the feeling of "No Comment" in the pendulum on the hand section. As you will recall, the pendulum is swinging freely as you are asking questions, and then comes to a grinding halt in which the pendulum just stops and is attracted to the center of your palm.

When you cast the pendulum, it's as if there is a magic gravitational pull that attracts the pendulum to the exact right location. The tip of the pendulum is pulled down and touches the paper. It finds the exact spot on the map or diagram, and then the tip of the pendulum feels like it is glued there. The body of the pendulum might fall to the left or right, but the tip stays fixated to the point on the map or diagram.

Casting the pendulum is an advanced technique and can be very difficult for beginners to feel for. Make sure you feel very confident about getting the pendulum to swing and move before you try to cast the pendulum onto a map or a diagram. Casting the pendulum is easier using a metal pendulum with an exact tip.

Maps can be used to help you decide on changing locations or finding things on a map. Traditionally in tribal communities, spiritual mystics might use casting to forecast where to plant crops, where severe weather might occur or where to find water. In our modern age we are concerned with moving to new locations or asking about "safe" locations if unpredictable events occur.

In my astral work, I have been asked to find things on a map. I have also been asked to pray for certain regions of the world, or create light grids over certain areas of the world. My intention here is to give the technique of casting. Each healer will be called upon by their angelic team if they want you to work with maps. You will be guided and you will know the questions to ask.

Diagrams can be more useful than charts for discussing anatomy and biological health. For example, you may want to dangle the pendulum over an anatomy chart and ask questions about your organs and body systems. As you advance in the practice, you might want to use diagrams out of books, rather than creating a chart. You can move through books or catalogs with the pendulum and get information by asking "Yes" or "No" questions. Casting the pendulum would give you the exact point on the map or diagram you are inquiring about.

This section is meant to give you the concept of the "casting" techniques. As you progress in the practice, allow your own curiosity to guide your questioning as you feel called to pull out a map or diagram to get more information. Remember this is an advanced skill, and not all lightworkers will be called to work with maps and diagrams. As your communication with your guidance team grows, you will be led intuitively to know if this is an activity that is useful to your healing and helping work.

Technique for Casting the Pendulum

First find the map or diagram that you want to use. I prefer to do this work on hard copy surfaces, but you could use it on a tablet computer surface. I personally use a hard copy surface to cast the pendulum on. Using the cell phone is not recommended. If you are using a cell phone application, it might be better to stick to using "Yes" and "No" questions rather than trying to find a specific location on the map or diagram.

Also for this work, a metal pendulum is highly recommended. The heavier the weight, the easier it will be to feel for the casting of the pendulum. This work is significantly harder if you are a beginner and try to use a crystal or lighter weight pendulum.

Let's work through an example together. I have provided three example maps, one of the United States, one of Europe and one of the World. These maps are divided into sections to help you narrow down the exact location for casting the pendulum. When you use your own maps, make sure to draw in grids which are demonstrated in the maps provided. This will narrow your search area.

Let's use the world map for our example. Ask that your guides show you a clockwise circle over the squared area of the map you should cast the pendulum over. Pendulum over each section within the map. For example with the world map, pendulum over the squared areas, 1/A, 1/B, 1/C, 1/D, keep going, 2/A, 2/B, 2/C, 2/D, keep going, until you cover all the areas on the map.

Once the pendulum makes a clockwise circle, you know what region the exact point will be on the map. Imagine that you got a clockwise circle over 1/B on the world map, which shows the United States. Next repeat the exercise again with the United States map. You receive the clockwise circle over the region 4/C on the US map. Now you have narrowed your search. Depending on your question and how specific you want to be, you might want to use a more detailed map to continue.

Once you have a smaller area to work with, hold the tip of the pendulum very close to the map or diagram, but not touching the surface. Move the pendulum back and forth slowly in a vertical or horizontal manner. Intend to "cast" the tip of the pendulum to the "exact point" on the map or diagram. This part is magical and hard to explain, but you will feel a pull downward, or your hand will naturally drop slightly, and the pendulum will anchor to the exact location on the map.

The action of the pendulum tip dropping is very subtle. Energetically and intuitively the reader holding the pendulum can feel it. The pendulum tip drops to touch the surface of the map and it feels like the tip of the pendulum is just stuck there or holding to that exact spot. The body of the pendulum may fall to either side, but the tip is anchored. Start by practicing on the maps that are provided.

Diagrams work the same way. Find a diagram you want to work with. Narrow the search by placing a simple grid pattern over the diagram to narrow the search area. Once the search is narrowed, cast the pendulum onto the diagram to find the exact location of what you are searching for.

I have provided an example chart of muscles of the back for you to practice with. You could ask questions like, "Which muscles in my back are injured?" or "Which area of my spine needs attention?" You can run the pendulum over a diagram of the body showing all the body to get more information on the health of your body. You can use any type of diagram and pendulum over it to get more exact information. I provide an anatomy diagram as an example to get you started. Have fun advancing your practice in this way!

LANGUAGE 3 CHARTS AND MAPS - US Map

LANGUAGE 3 CHARTS AND MAPS - Europe

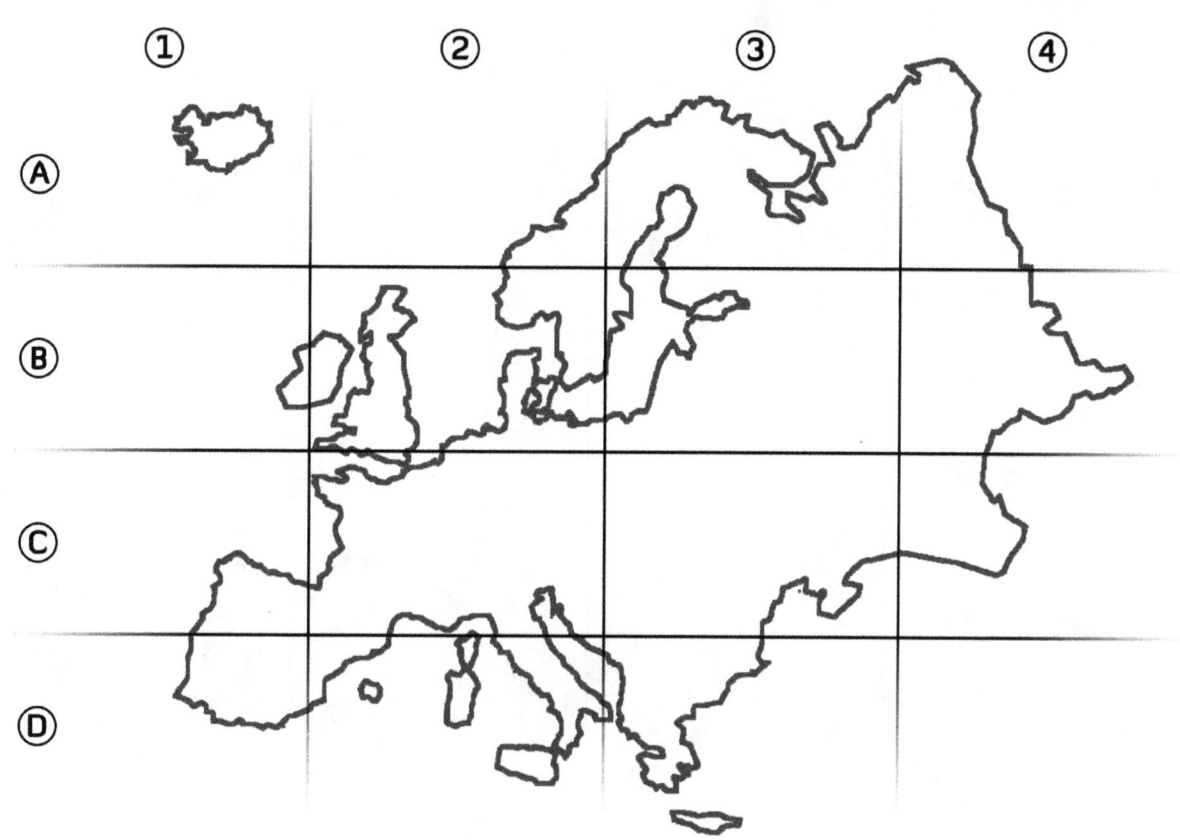

LANGUAGE 3 CHARTS AND MAPS - World Map

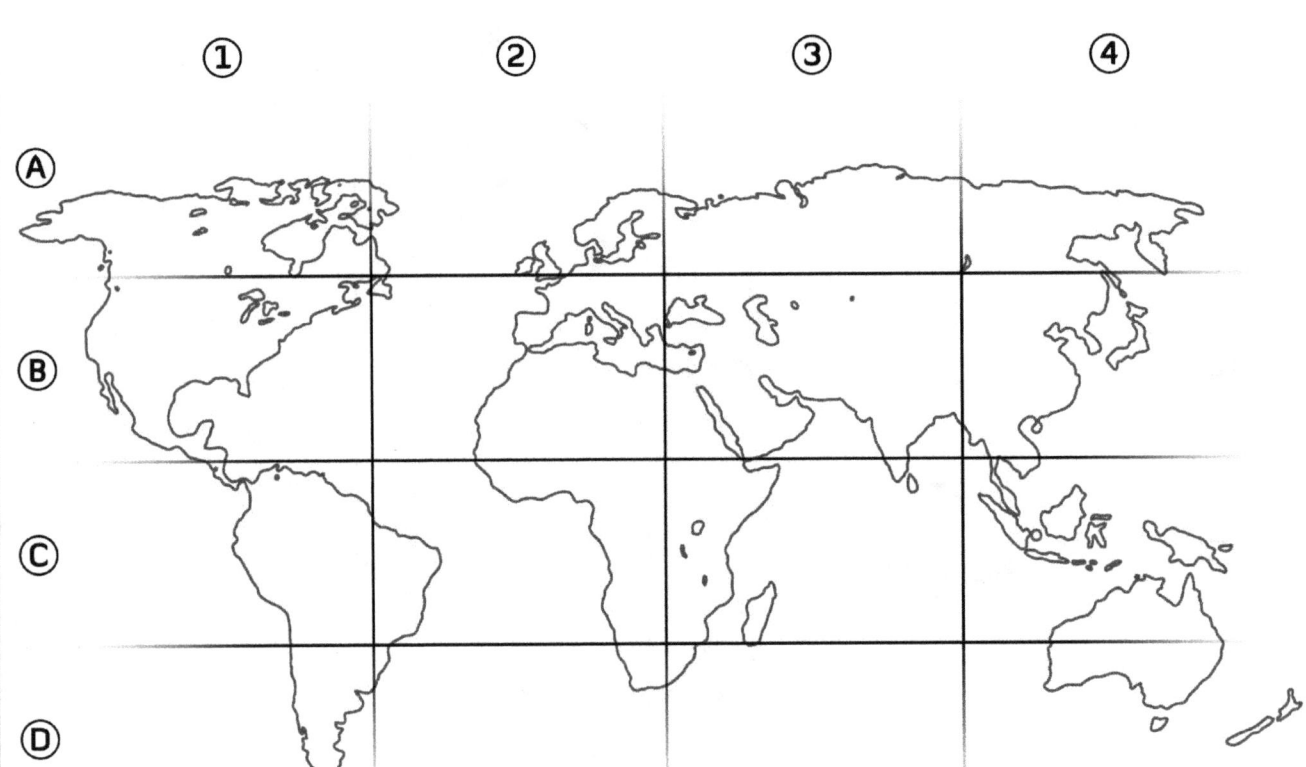

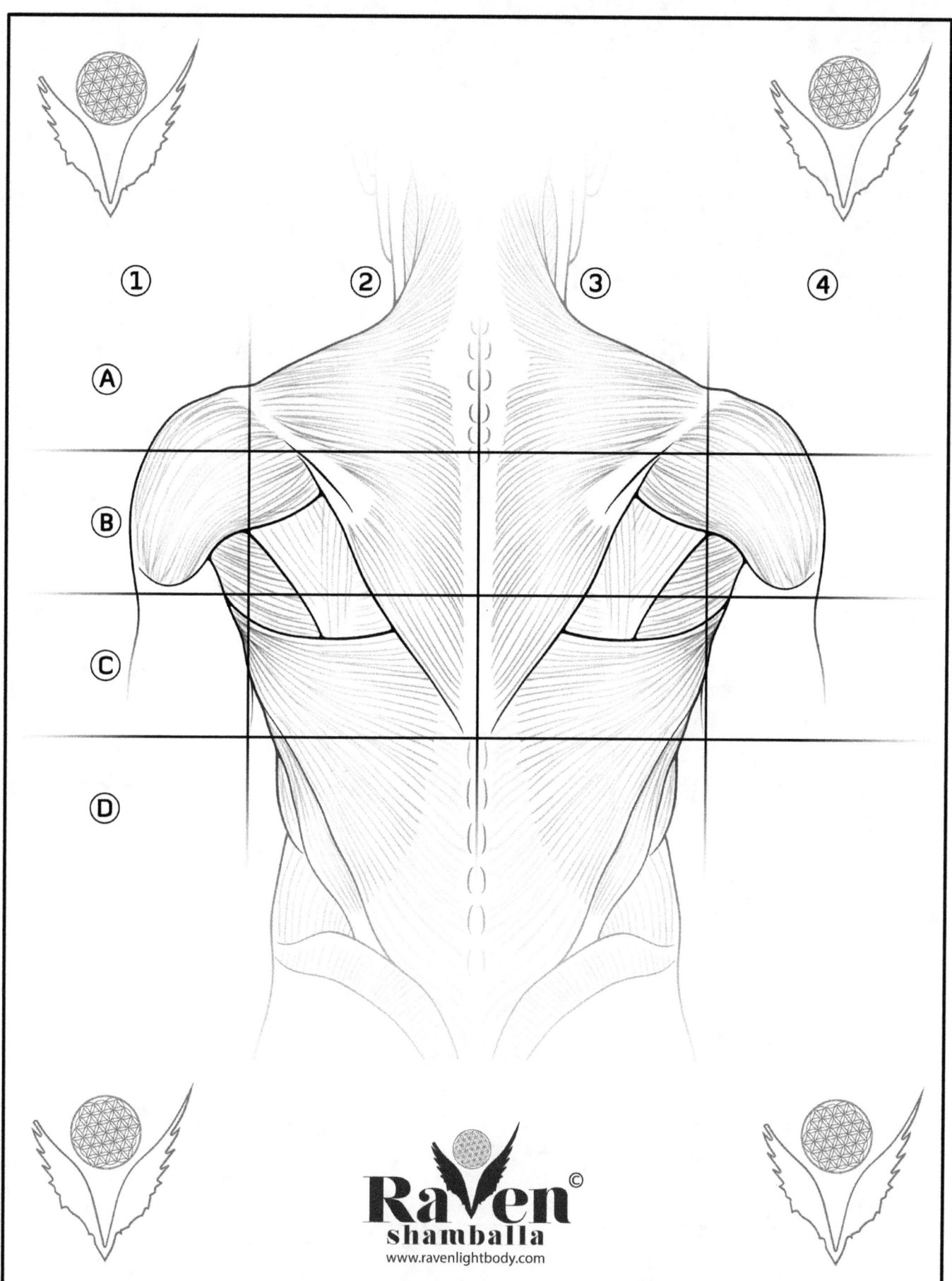

NOTES

CPSIA information can be obtained
at www.ICGtesting.com
Printed in the USA
BVHW011651240921
617289BV00010B/613